THE SOUTH WALES MAIN LINE

PART THREE
CARDIFF (WEST) TO BRIDGEND

BY

JOHN HODGE

Landore 'Castle' No. 7016 *Chester Castle* accelerating away from Cardiff General station with the down 'South Wales Pullman', 8.50 a.m. Paddington, in October 1958. The engine had worked the service from Paddington, with a crew change at Newport from Old Oak to Ebbw Jct (Monday) or Landore men (Tuesday to Friday). Landore Turn 3 engine worked both the up (4.30 p.m. Swansea) and down Pullman trains in the winter 1958/9 schedules. R. O. TUCK

WILD SWAN PUBLICATIONS

ISBN 1 874103 95 X

Designed by Paul Karau
Printed by Amadeus Press, Cleckheaton

Published by
WILD SWAN PUBLICATIONS LTD.
1-3 Hagbourne Road, Didcot, Oxon, OX11 8DP

DEDICATION

I dedicate this book to my late parents, Arthur Percival and Doris Lilian Hodge. My father died in 1974, aged 73, but my mother lived on for another 20 years and finally departed in 1995, at the ripe old age of 93, just failing to reach her 94th. We enjoyed a good home life at Barry from 1942, having moved there from Risca in the Western Valley for the benefit of my father's health. I am grateful to both for putting up with my passion for railways during the period I lived at our Barry home until 1970, and for finding the resources to put me through a Grammar School and University education, which stood me in good stead thereafter during my railway career which lasted from 1961 to 1992.

ACKNOWLEDGEMENTS

I would like to thank John Copsey and Richard Woodley for their help with captions and text. R. A. Cooke's invaluable Track Layout Diagrams have been widely consulted.

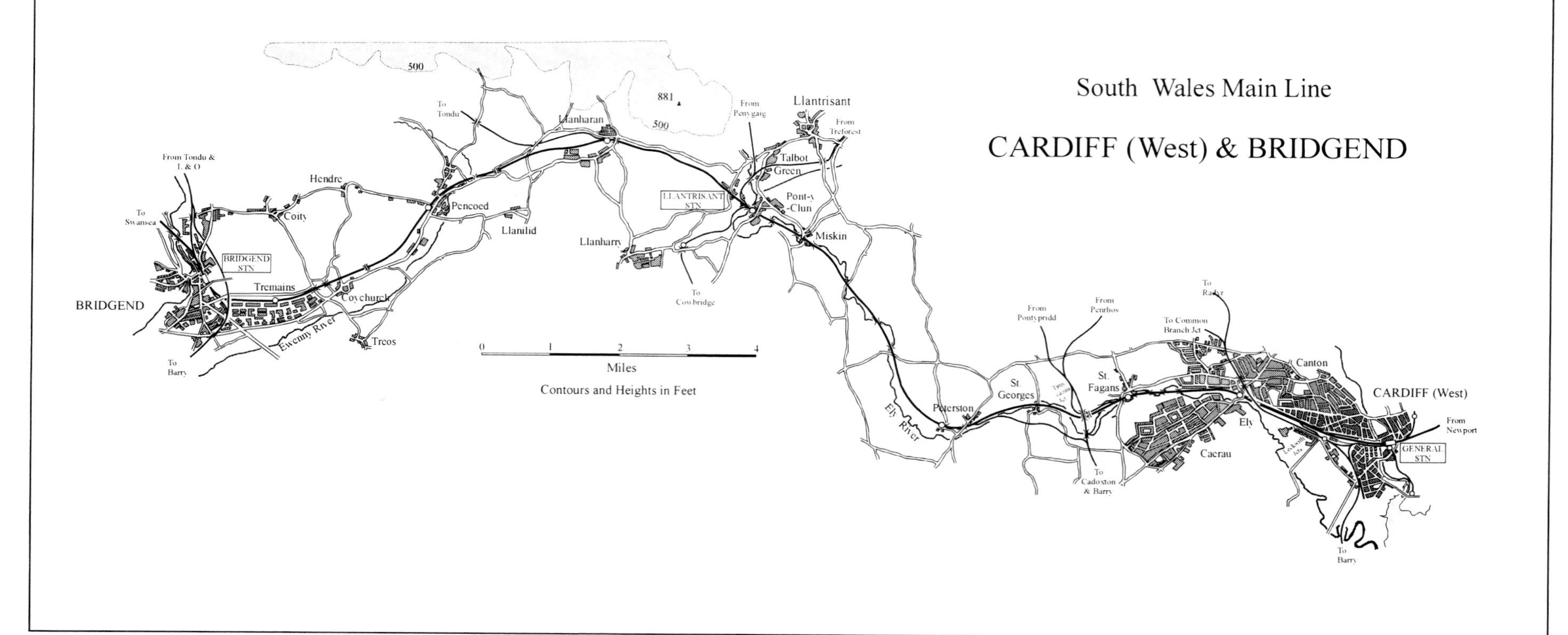

The evening sun at St. Fagans favoured photographs of down trains from the north side. The picturesque nature of this country station, with the station house seen at the end of the up platform, is well illustrated in this photograph of Llanelly's '42XX' No. 5230 heading west with a down 'F' class mixed freight on Saturday, 20th June 1959. The cattle dock line behind the up platform was by now heavily overgrown.

PREFACE

The section of line from Cardiff to Bridgend held great interest for me photographically, being within reasonable distance, even by bicycle, of my home at Barry. I regularly cycled out to St. Fagans to witness the speeding expresses and rumbling goods trains crossing over the River Ely and the level crossing, where the crossing gates were opened and closed and the signals pulled off and restored so often that one wondered whether the signal box was manned by an octopus!

My collection of photographs at St. Fagans must be one of the largest (if not *the* largest) available. My aim in producing this book is to show as many individual locations as possible along the section of line concerned, using my own and, largely, Bob Tuck's collection of photographs. Bob used to frequent the area around the former Barry Railway Viaduct, between St. Fagans and St. George's, and it is his photographs which cover this location as I never used that vantage point; conversely, he hardly ever photographed at St. Fagans station.

I found that my old friend Sid Rickard, who photographed widely in South Wales during the 1950s, had taken quite a few shots around Ely, the first station west of Cardiff General, and Brian Miller, who now owns Sid's collection, has very kindly provided a good selection of these, to complement my own shots at Ely, thus providing a comprehensive coverage of this interesting, and previously little seen, location.

Even putting together the large number of photographs of the Cardiff & Bridgend section available in my own, Bob Tuck and Sid Rickard's collections, I still found there were several 'black holes' not covered, and I had recourse to the various national dealers to see what they were holding. I am very grateful to Roger Carpenter for providing quite a few views of stations along the line which help significantly in providing a fuller coverage of the section. I am also grateful to Brian Stephenson for permission to use photographs from the Bob Tuck collection, which now forms part of Rail Archive Stephenson, and also to Michael Hale for amplifying coverage from his excellent South Wales collection.

During my time working for the Cardiff District and Cardiff Divisional Offices from 1961–70, I was partly responsible for train running along the line from Cardiff to Bridgend, when with the Cardiff District Train Office from 1961–63. I saw first hand the problems created by inadequate line capacity, and it came as no surprise when, in advance of Beeching, the Cardiff Office decided to withdraw facilities from the smaller stations along the line in the cause of speeding-up the freight services which earned vastly more than did stopping passenger trains. However, as the big wheel of history continues to turn, we have seen some stations restored, and a new local service from Maesteg to Cardiff introduced from 1992, which would have been absolutely unheard of during the heyday of heavy freight in the 1960s and 70s. The South Wales freight scene is now but a shadow of what it was even in the final decade of steam operation, and I hope that this book will present to the reader a good impression of what sights were to be beheld along the line fifty years ago.

John Hodge

A turn-of-the-century view of Cardiff General, taken from the luggage conveyor which spanned the backs at the west end of the platforms until the station was rebuilt and new underground connections and lifts installed in the 1934 modernisation. On the extreme right of the picture, a bay platform (where platform No. 7 was later created) can be seen standing empty; this was provided under the 1896 rebuilding and was not shown with a platform number, so presumably was used for parcels vans, with access (as can be seen) on either side to also serve Riverside Station to the south. Platforms 6 and 4, both then used the for Valleys trains, were unoccupied when this picture was taken, but a 3- or 4-coach train of clerestory stock is seen in bay platform 5, forming a westward departure. At platform 3 – the down main platform – we can see a 2–4–0 at the head of a train of some 8 coaches. The down through line was clear, but the empty stock standing on the up through, consisting of a horsebox, clerestory coach and a 'Siphon' van, would doubtless soon be removed. The up main platform (No. 2) was occupied by a four-coach passenger train with a further four vehicles on the rear forming tail traffic, including an open wagon. The *Western Mail* newspaper offices are significant in their original position on the left of the picture. The 1896 works at Cardiff significantly provided the flyover to carry trains to and from Queen Street and the Valleys, replacing the previous conventional double junction off the main lines.

COLLECTION P. Q. TRELOAR

INTRODUCTION

The famous picture of Bridgend station, looking west, dating from about 1904, with Barry Railway Class 'J' 2–4–2T No. 97 standing in the Barry bay with a return train to Barry. The class 'Js' were built between 1897 and 1899, and were the Barry's main passenger engines, working to Cardiff, Pontypridd and Bridgend. They were renumbered from 86–91 and 94–98 to 1311–1321 by the GWR in 1922, and were withdrawn between 1926 and 1930. The double-headed main line train at the up main platform, was headed by 'Bulldog' No. 3422 *Sir John Llewellyn* (which became No. 3370 after the renumbering of 28th December 1912). This engine was based at New Milford from new in March 1903 until entering Swindon for her first general repair in July 1904, following which she was allocated to Swindon, so this picture would seem to have been taken between those dates. The train engine appears to have been a 'Duke'. A train from the Bridgend Valleys is seen at the other platform, headed by an 0–6–0 saddle tank.

LENS OF SUTTON

The 20 miles 18 chains between Cardiff General and Bridgend was a crucial section of the South Wales Main Line, quite different in nature from the line to the east of Cardiff, which was progressively quadrupled over the whole of its length from Severn Tunnel Junction. The section westwards from Cardiff remained largely double track only, presenting continual regulation problems, with control exercised by the signalmen making best use of the many loops which existed along the route; the aim was to avoid delay to the passenger and the higher-class freight services, while ensuring that the general goods trains were able to proceed at a reasonable pace.

The broad-gauge South Wales Railway was opened from Chepstow to Swansea in 1850. In general terms, the section from Cardiff to Bridgend was the easiest section to construct, with no serious obstacles to encompass, and no tunnels required. However, a straight line of rails between the two places was impossible due to the many necessary crossings of the rivers, avoidance of the higher ground, and other deviations to be negotiated, together with subsidence caused by underground workings in some areas. The result was a line with a multitude of curves and underbridges, which were to cause continual maintenance problems on this two-track route in years to come.

In 1850, the timetable showed only four passenger trains per day between Cardiff and Bridgend, departing Cardiff at 9.15 a.m., 1.5 p.m., 5.30 p.m. and 8.15 p.m., arriving at Bridgend an hour later, except for the 5.30 p.m. which was a faster service and did not call at Llantrisant. On Sundays, two services ran at 8.15 a.m. and 7.15 p.m. from Cardiff. In the return direction on weekdays, four services operated from Bridgend at 8.10 a.m., 11.32 a.m., 3.10 p.m. and 7.10 p.m., with an 8.10 a.m. and 7.10 p.m. on Sundays, the normal journey time being 58 minutes. At this time, there were intermediate stations at Ely, St. Fagans, Llantrisant and Pencoed.

Continual problems existed in the area due to the incompatibility of broad and narrow gauges. In 1860, the Ely Valley company put a Bill through Parliament to change their gauge from broad to narrow, and construct a separate line from Llantrisant to Cardiff alongside the SWR broad-gauge line. The SWR offered to lay a mixed-gauge line themselves, but the GWR refused to sanction this and the Ely Valley company's scheme fell through.

Along with the rest of the main line between Swindon and Milford, the Cardiff & Bridgend section was converted from broad to narrow gauge during May 1872.

As the volume of traffic built up, especially in the period when coal traffic began to reach a very significant level, it became necessary to install loops at strategic points, the previous method of allowing a following train to pass having been to shunt the train in front into a siding or onto a branch. The first loop between Bridgend and Cardiff was installed at Peterston in 1896, with up and down loop lines laid outside the up and down main lines, particularly to facilitate the handling of traffic for exchange with the Barry Railway. As South Wales coal traffic reached record levels just before the First World War, three further sets of loops were added in 1914, at Pencoed (up), Miskin to Pontsarn (up and down) and St. Fagans (down). Three more were added in the early 1920s, at Llantrisant (up and down in 1920), at Llanharan (up and down in 1921) and at Pencoed (down in 1923). Finally, with the opening of Bridgend Industrial Estate at Tremains, up and down loops were installed there in 1938. The up and down loops between Miskin and Pontsarn were of exceptional length, nearly 1¼ miles long, capable of holding 4 trains each of 60 wagons, including engine and van; they were reduced in length at the east end in 1966 by 34 chains, being cut back to their pre-1922 termination point west of the river bridge at Duffryn Bridge, where there was previously a signal box until 1922 when it was

Llantrisant in the early years of the last century, looking west, when the station had been named 'Lantrisent' by the photographer; 19th century service documents show an earlier spelling of 'Llantrissant', though they dropped an 's' as the 20th century approached. The station staff had been posed for the shot together with a few passengers of the day. The separate bracket signal on the left controlled the exit from the south face of the down island platform to the Cowbridge, main and yard/Penygraig lines, with the down main line signal off for the Penygraig and Pontypridd branch.

AUTHOR'S COLLECTION

replaced by Pontsarn Crossing box. The Peterston loops had central connections to allow higher category freight services to overtake lower category.

The Cardiff & Bridgend section enjoyed the same maximum line speed of 75 mph as that from Severn Tunnel to Cardiff during the 1950s and 60s. However, there were 60mph permanent restrictions over curves for a mile through St. Fagans, and for ¼ mile at Peterston. There was also a long-standing ¼ mile subsidence slack to 40 mph just to the west of Llanharan.

In the mid-1950s, freight services over the Section were heavy, with some fifty booked trains in each direction daily. Whilst the thirty or so passenger services each way were very largely confined to the 8.0 a.m. to 8.0 p.m. period, the timetabled freight trains were equally divided, with 25 each way during those hours, and 25 in each direction overnight between 8.0 p.m. and 8.0 a.m., but additional services ran under Control orders.

The increasing level of traffic, both passenger and goods, made the line a difficult one to operate in both directions, and maximum use was made of the loops for regulation purposes. The problem was worse in the up direction as goods trains were normally fully loaded eastwards, whereas often empty westwards, producing slower speeds in the up direction. The passenger traffic levels, during the years with which photographs in this book deal, can be exemplified by this listing of Saturdays Excepted services from the Summer 1957 *Working Time Table.*

Hours	*00–06*		*06–14*		*14–00*	
	Down	*Up*	*Down*	*Up*	*Down*	*Up*
Express Passenger	3	0	8	12	10	9
Stopping Passenger	0	0	5	3	6	6
Parcels	1	1	1	1	1	2
Milk/Empties	2	0	0	0	1	4
Fish/Empties	1	0	1	0	0	1

The extremely low level of passenger-rated activity on the up line during the night is very noticeable, track capacity during these hours being devoted almost exclusively to freight services. The one up night service was the 7.50 p.m. Neyland to Cardiff Parcels, at Bridgend from 1.53 until 2.10 a.m., arriving Cardiff General at 2.45 a.m. The next up passenger-rated service was the 3.55 a.m. boat train from Fishguard Harbour to Paddington, which passed Bridgend at 6.28 a.m.

After the Grouping in 1922, some relief was afforded to the Cardiff to Bridgend section by using the line via Barry and the Vale of Glamorgan as a diversionary route when the main line was blocked by planned engineering work or derailment, with a few services being routed that way in some timetables to relieve volume at critical times.

In the down direction, trains leaving Cardiff had a relatively easy run up the Ely Valley as far as Llantrisant, but between there and Llanharan, the highest point on this section of line, they faced a stiffer climb at 1 in 106 before enjoying a downhill stretch through Pencoed along the Ewenny Valley, followed by a run on the level into Bridgend. In the up direction, there was a climb from west of Pencoed to Llanharan, the steepest point occurring on the approach to Llanharan with an incline of 1 in 138, then 126. However, once 'over the top' at Llanharan, there was a lovely 13½ mile run downhill, or on the level, all the way to the outskirts of Cardiff.

The regulation problem was compounded by the fact that there were now six intermediate stations between Cardiff General and Bridgend. Ely (Main Line) station, 2½ miles west of Cardiff General, was intended as a means of enabling the local community to travel speedily into the city by train, but convenience dominated and the community mostly travelled in by tram, bus and, later, trolleybus, affording better access to the city centre, leading to the rundown in use of the station and its ultimate demise. Then followed two rural stations, firstly St. Fagans, which became the epitome of a country station, and then Peterston. St. Fagans was also the point at which the Barry Railway connected with the GWR by means of a line from Tynycaeau Junction on their main line from Cadoxton to Pontypridd and Trehafod. The Barry built their own nest of sidings to the west of the station, where they had their own signal box and goods shed. Their Chairman, the Earl of Plymouth, had his own private platform, located just behind the site of the GWR signal box. The amalgamation of the Barry Railway with the Great Western ended the need for separate facilities and these were gradually removed, though it was 1950 before all the sidings went.

Peterston was another rural station, but in operating terms, like St. Fagans, it was a key junction with the Barry Railway and was the point at which up line traffic from Llantrisant was exchanged with the Barry for conveyance on to Cadoxton and Barry Docks, traffic from Bridgend and west travelling over the Vale of Glamorgan line. Though this all became GWR traffic from the grouping, and though the amount of traffic passing via Peterston declined, it was 1964 before these sidings and their relative connections into and out of the main lines were removed.

Llantrisant Station, just over 11 miles from Cardiff, drew much of its passenger traffic from Pontyclun and surrounding villages, for which it became a railhead in both passenger and goods terms, with its own goods shed for sundries traffic, and engine shed with both local and main-line duties. It was the main station between Cardiff and Bridgend, and its importance was accentuated by the fact it was a major freight junction for coal, and later coke, traffic, emanating from collieries such as Cwm, Coedely, Gilfach Goch, etc, the first two also developing large coke ovens. Branch passenger services also ran from Llantrisant to Pontypridd, Penygraig, Cowbridge and Aberthaw, with associated goods workings, all being gradually discontinued by the end of the 1950s. The transfer of the Royal Mint to the area in the early 1960s failed to prevent the station from being closed to passenger traffic in 1964. However, a new station at Pontyclun was opened in 1992, served by the new Maesteg to Cardiff DMU Service.

Two and a half miles west of Llantrisant was the junction station of Llanharan, from where a branch line ran to Tondu, giving access to Tondu yard from the north end and enabling goods trains from Cardiff to use the branch to obviate the need for turning tender engines which then ran south at Tondu, returning to Cardiff via Bridgend.

The large village of Pencoed was the next passenger station westwards, and, though this was closed in 1964, it has also re-opened to be served by the new Maesteg to Cardiff service. Tremains Platform was opened in 1938 to serve the Bridgend Industrial Estate.

The problems caused by insufficient line capacity and growing heavy freight traffic, especially oil traffic from the West Wales refineries, required a high-level review of the section of line between Cardiff and Bridgend in the early 1960s when it was decided to withdraw passenger facilities from all intermediate stations, including Llantrisant, and this was effected in 1962/64. Though goods and general freight yards remained at several stations, these were progressively withdrawn under coal concentration schemes for house coal traffic. Concentration of goods and collected/delivered freight at either Cardiff or Bridgend Goods, ultimately at Cardiff only, was also effected during the mid and late 1960s.

All types of Western Region locomotives, except 'Kings' and '47XXs', were permitted to work over the Cardiff to Bridgend section. Though 'Kings' were cleared to work as far west as Cardiff in 1959, they were still restricted beyond, due to the many underbridges crossing the Ely River. Close proximity of the trackbed to the river and the succession of bridges made this an expensive and difficult section of line to maintain, often resulting in Sunday diversions via the Vale of Glamorgan.

Travelling over the line in a modern High Speed Train, or even a second or third generation DMU, affords little idea of what the level of activity was before the closure of stations and yards, signal boxes, collieries, etc., but we are fortunate in being able to put together a comprehensive picture still through the activities of those of us who recorded the scene on film for posterity.

This view shows Severn Tunnel Junction 2–8–0 No. 3835 taking advantage of occupancy of the down main with all signals off as it accelerated past the west end of Canton depot with a down class 'D' express freight, probably from Severn Tunnel Yard to Margam or Llandilo Jct in September 1960. At this time, at least one third of the wagons on the class 'D' freights were attached to the vacuum braking system, and the train ran at a maximum speed of 45 m.p.h. In addition to the varied selection of vans, some open or flat wagons are seen marshalled in the centre and at the rear of the train.

CANTON WEST

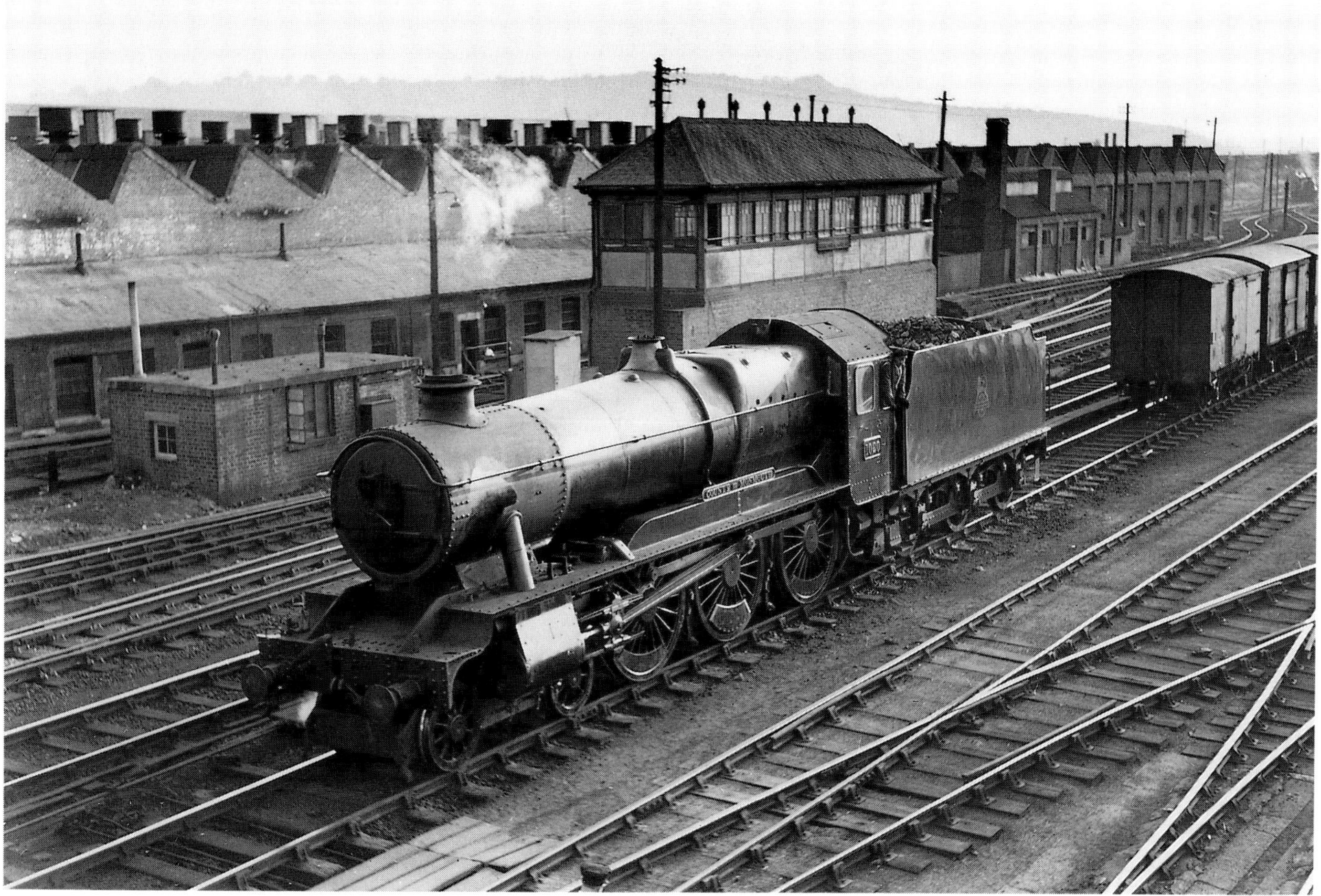

Neyland 'Counties' usually worked only as far east as Cardiff, other than when destined for overhaul at Swindon works. This picture taken on Monday, 25th July 1955, shows No. 1020, *County of Monmouth* moving forward off the 3.50 p.m. Milford Haven to Weymouth fish outside Canton Siding box, from where the train would be taken forward by a Westbury 'Hall'. Though the 'Counties' proved a problematical engine for main-line express services, they performed well in Cornwall and West Wales where their power proved beneficial, especially on heavy class 'C' services over the curving and undulating routes. Neyland was allocated three 'Counties' in October 1948 (Nos. 1001/09/20), and these were joined by Nos. 1027 and 1029 in November 1950 and December 1953 respectively. R.O. TUCK

The 11.10 am. Milford Haven to Paddington (3.0 p.m. from Cardiff) passing the west end of Canton shed on Saturday, 24th September 1960 behind Old Oak Common Castle No. 5087 *Tintern Abbey*. For the engine, this was the return working of the previous day's 6.55 p.m. Paddington to Fishguard, which Old Oak Common engine and men worked to Swansea, the men lodging overnight. The engine had just passed the Canton Sidings down starter, whilst the end of the train is seen passing the up home signals for the up main and relief lines.

It was very rare indeed for an Aberystwyth engine to work through to Cardiff, but one occasion on which this would happen was for soccer internationals at Ninian Park. It might have been expected that a 'Manor' would be provided for such occasions, but here '43XX' 2–6–0 No. 6378 worked special No. 023, passing Canton on the final mile into Cardiff General during September 1960. Canton '43XXs' did, however, work regularly to Aberystwyth on a diagram shared with Carmarthen: this began with the 9.45 p.m. Cardiff (Newtown) to Carmarthen goods (MWF), continuing the following day with the 10.45 a.m. Carmarthen to Aberystwyth and 5.40 p.m. Aberystwyth to Carmarthen passenger trains, finally returning with the 11.35 p.m. Carmarthen to Cardiff goods (TThS).

Soon after receiving a 'Heavy' overhaul at Swindon, Old Oak Common 'Castle' No. 4078 *Pembroke Castle* is seen heading westwards out of Cardiff past Canton depot with the 11.55 a.m. Paddington to Pembroke Dock service in September 1960. The engine was carrying reporting number 'F23' instead of the correct 'F32', a mistake that happened on more than one occasion, possibly due to incorrect information being given to the crew; 'F23' denoted the 10.0 a.m. Birmingham to Cardiff service in the summer timetable. The trailing connection in the down relief in the foreground gave access to/from the shed, whilst Canton mileage yard, on the other side of the running lines, served the western side of the city. Wagons of house coal for local merchants can be seen, whilst the London Brick Company received many wagons of bricks there. A rake of empty parcel vans, as seen in the background, could often be seen shunted into the yard, either to make up a train to be worked away or to supply vans for Sherman's football pools traffic from the former Canton milk depot.

Passing between the Canton Sidings up main and up relief home signals, Landore 'Castle' No. 7012 *Barry Castle* is seen with the 11.10 a.m. Milford Haven to Paddington ('A90'; 3.0 p.m. from Cardiff) during September 1960 on the approach to Cardiff General station. The trailing connections into Canton shed and across the main lines to the up relief, for use in changing engines, were protected by the reversing signal, complete with indicator panel.

Long-term Landore 'Castle' No. 5051 *Earl Bathurst* (now preserved at Didcot) passing Canton depot with the 11.55 a.m. Paddington to Pembroke Dock express during the summer of 1960. The opens visible in Canton mileage yard would probably have been connected with brick traffic for the London Brick Company.

LECKWITH JUNCTION

Reference was made in Volume 1 to the large-scale alterations to layout and new construction made at Cardiff by the Great Western Railway between 1931–34 to remove the bottleneck conditions through the station with relief lines being created through from a new junction at Leckwith, west of Canton depot. Leckwith Junction signal box was located at 171 m 49ch, controlling not only the entrance and exit to and from the new running loops and also the main line, but a new junction which took eastbound trains in a south-east direction through Ninian Park platform (for Association Football traffic), then providing access to the west end of Canton carriage depot, which was considerably enlarged under the 1931–34 replanning, and linking with Penarth Curve North and South for trains to Barry and Penarth, and Penarth Curve East for trains for Cardiff General, thus creating an alternative route to the main line, though for many years little used as such.

At Leckwith Junction South, the line joined the former Taff Vale Railway line from Radyr Junction just to the west of Ninian Park Platform. Between the main line and Leckwith Junction South the line was double, but was singled in 1966, the down line being retained. The route from Penarth Curve East through Ninian Park to Radyr has subsequently been used by the Cardiff City line DMU service, which commenced in more recent years. The creation of the new Leckwith Junction box in 1931 enabled the former small boxes at Moors Lane (172m 16ch) and Ely Paper Mills Crossing (172m 28ch) to be closed, this creating a throughout block post between the new box and Ely Main Line SB, located at the west end of that station platform. The former TVR line climbed westwards en route to Radyr to cross the main line just to the east of the Paper Mills installation, with connections providing access to the works from both the branch and main lines.

Leckwith Junction North gave access (via Leckwith Jct. South) to the ex-Taff Vale line from Radyr to Penarth Curve North, East and South. The first provided entry to Canton carriage depot, the second provided an alternative route to Cardiff General, whilst the third gave access to the Barry line, and was used for excursions to Barry Island from Llantrisant and stations west (after the closure of the former Barry Railway's Peterston line) to avoid using the Vale of Glamorgan line, and also having to reverse at Barry Town for the Barry Island branch. Here, the 11.10 a.m. Milford Haven is seen passing Leckwith Jct. North behind a returning Old Oak Common double-chimney 'Castle'. From September 1961, the title 'Capitals United Express' was transferred onto the 8.55 a.m. Paddington to West Wales and the 11.10 a.m. Milford Haven to Paddington, having previously been carried by the 6.30 a.m. Swansea and 3.55 p.m. Paddington trains.

With Leckwith Junction North signal box visible at the end of the train, Canton 'Britannia' No. 70029 *Shooting Star* is seen passing the southern suburbs of Canton with the 1.55 pm. Paddington to Pembroke Dock service (Train No. 169) during the summer of 1956. The engine started the day with the 8.0 am. Cardiff to Paddington (6.30 a.m. Swansea), and was now working from Paddington through to Swansea, from where it would return with the 9.10 pm. Swansea to Cardiff. At approx. 390 miles, this was one of the longest engine turns on the WR at that time, and it was not unknown for the tender to be virtually empty of coal by the time the 338 miles to Swansea had been covered. S. RICKARD

Just before milepost 172½, the main line passed under the former Taff Vale Railway's Penarth Curve to Radyr line, a goods route which in Great Western days carried trains between the Cardiff yards or Barry and Radyr (for the Valleys). By the time of this photograph, in 1953, it was used for similar regular freight services, football specials to Ninian Park, plus a few excursions to Barry Island, but later formed the nucleus of the Cardiff City line, also being used to create through circular DMU working from and to the Valleys. A detailed view of the Radyr line is afforded by this shot of Canton 'Mogul' No. 6333 heading for one of the Cardiff yards with an eastbound class 'J' freight, probably from Tondu or Llantrisant, on 5th February 1953. Both the main and ex-Taff lines were connected with Ely Paper Mills, seen in the left background. The neatness of the allotments on the left contrasts with the decrepit state of the buildings on the right, which look as if they were in the process of demolition.

S. RICKARD

ELY MAIN LINE

Approaching Ely station from the east, the double-track main line borders the River Ely to its south side for a short distance, while to the north side of the line is the Cardiff to Swansea A48 trunk road; this crosses the line at the east end of Ely Main Line station platforms en route to the city boundary at Culverhouse Cross. Following the crossovers providing access to the Ely Paper Mills (later Wiggins Teape) sidings, from where in the 1950s a through class 'F' train of vans of paper ran to Woodford, hauled by a Canton WD 2–8–0, there was a connection from the up main to a siding running behind the down platform into the mileage yard, which also had a connection into the down main at the west end of that yard.

The main mileage yard traffic in later years at least was domestic coal for local merchants, but in former times it had also contained a horse-loading dock, authorised in 1927 for handling horses at local races. With the planning for the high-cost Multiple Aspect Signalling (MAS) Scheme in 1964, all such small mileage yards in the area were closed, and the domestic coal traffic was concentrated at Virgil Street, Grangetown, which was entered via Penarth Curve North. The station itself was closed to passenger traffic in September 1962 as part of a plan to improve line speed for freight services by removing stopping passenger trains, which yielded little revenue.

On the up side at Ely was a brewery, which changed ownership several times during the existence of the railway. Traffic for the brewery was placed on an up siding west of the signal box, the siding being shown as extended in 1885, and the brewery owned by Messrs. Showell in 1899. In October 1900, a new Private Siding Agreement was taken out in the name of Crosswells Cardiff Brewery, terminated in May 1961, though, as can be seen from the photographs, the up siding was still in situ in 1964, though removed under the MAS alterations. The site of the brewery (which used the most effective slogan of 'Ely Ales, Best in Wales') is now a housing estate.

This second view, from the same vantage point, shows Landore 'Castle' No. 4074 *Caldicot Castle*, with Hawksworth tender, was heading a stopping service from Swansea to Cardiff formed of a four-coach set plus two vans as tail traffic. S. RICKARD

Hall
FINCHLEY ROAD
BROOK ROAD
Foot Bridge
Brewery
L.B.
P.H.
ELY ROAD
S.B.
Vinegar Brewery
Station
WROUGHTON STREET
Station Terrace
W.M.
S.Post
COWBRIDGE ROAD
Ely Brewery
COWBRIDGE ROAD A.48
Def.
S.P.
956 3.859
Party Boro. & Ward Bdy.
Def.
Foot Bridge
C.R.
953 ·401
Ely River (Afon Lai) 954 2.865
955 ·393
957 ·718
Reservoir
988 ·205
Ely Bridge
Riverside Terrace
Riverside Ter.
P.O.
BM.32·8
T.C.B.
958 ·507
R.C. Church

The 3.25 p.m. Cardiff to Swansea five-coach, all stations stopper, hauled by Ebbw Jct. 'Grange' No. 6838 *Goodmoor Grange*, is seen slowing down for a stop at Ely Main Line station on Monday, 16th June 1958. This train started from bay platform No. 5 at Cardiff General, and was formed with the stock off the 1.0 p.m. Gloucester, which arrived at platform No. 4 and was then shunted into the bay. The list of stations called out by the train announcer at Cardiff would now sound like a piece of history: 'Ely, St. Fagans, Peterston, Llantrisant, Llanharan, Pencoed, Bridgend, Pyle, Port Talbot, Briton Ferry, Neath, Skewen, Llansamlet, Landore and Swansea.' Only four stations now survive between the two cities.

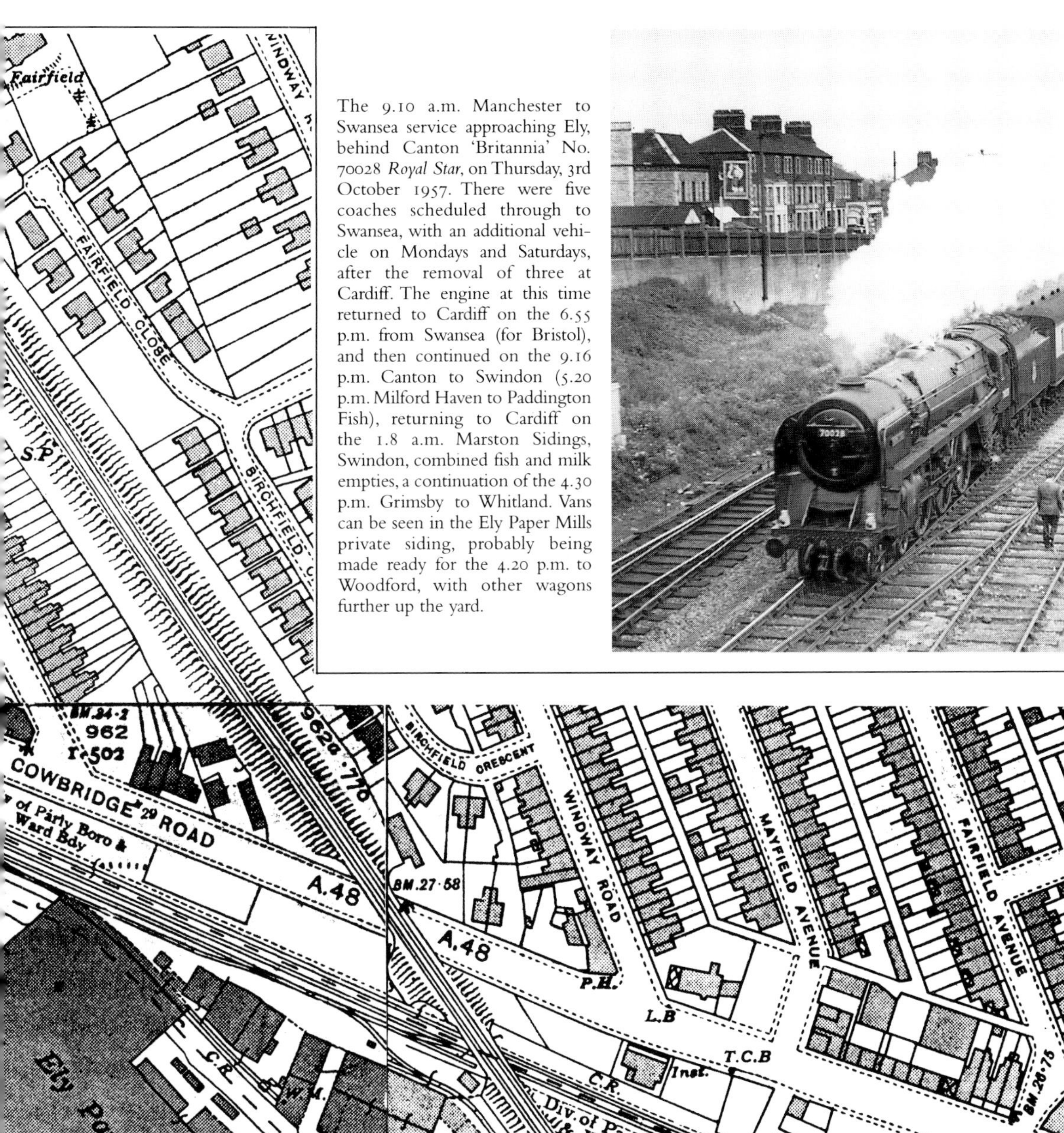

The 9.10 a.m. Manchester to Swansea service approaching Ely, behind Canton 'Britannia' No. 70028 *Royal Star*, on Thursday, 3rd October 1957. There were five coaches scheduled through to Swansea, with an additional vehicle on Mondays and Saturdays, after the removal of three at Cardiff. The engine at this time returned to Cardiff on the 6.55 p.m. from Swansea (for Bristol), and then continued on the 9.16 p.m. Canton to Swindon (5.20 p.m. Milford Haven to Paddington Fish), returning to Cardiff on the 1.8 a.m. Marston Sidings, Swindon, combined fish and milk empties, a continuation of the 4.30 p.m. Grimsby to Whitland. Vans can be seen in the Ely Paper Mills private siding, probably being made ready for the 4.20 p.m. to Woodford, with other wagons further up the yard.

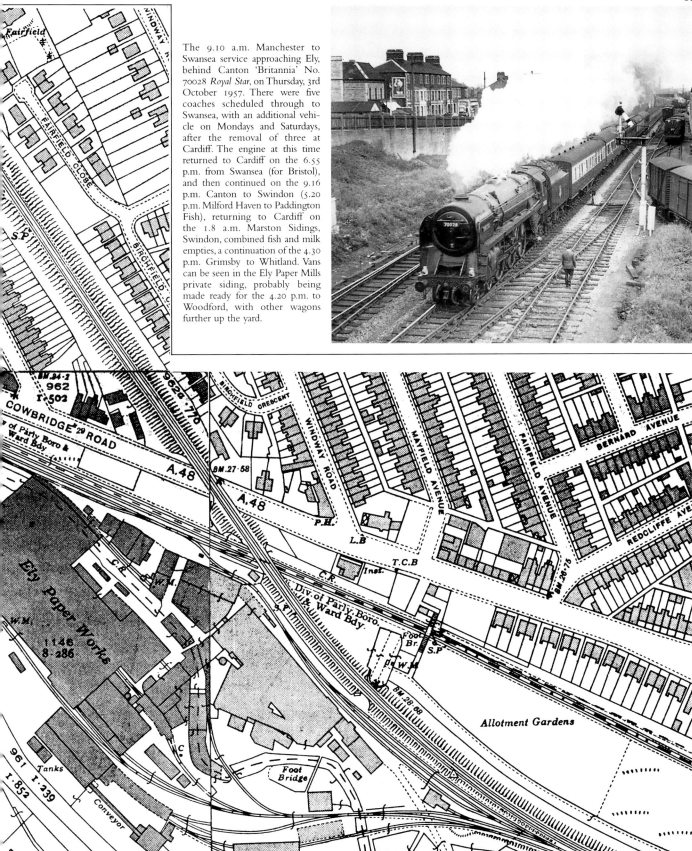

Taken from 25-inch Ordnance Survey for 1940. (Crown copyright reserved)

Having just passed under the bridge carrying the A48 trunk road from Cardiff to Swansea – which continued behind the fence across the centre of the picture – Ebbw Jct. '5101' class 2–6–2T No. 5173 is seen here with the summertime only 2.20 p.m. (SX) Porthcawl to Cardiff on Monday, 16th June 1958, balanced off the 12.15 pm. Newport to Porthcawl. On Saturdays, this train started at 12.20 p.m. from Cardiff, and returned there as the 2.0 p.m. Porthcawl. The formation in the late 1950s was shown as a five-coach corridor set on weekdays, replaced by a five-coach non-corridor rake and a three-coach corridor set on Saturdays.

Canton 'Hall' No. 6932 *Burwarton Hall*, paired with a Hawksworth straight-sided tender, approaching Ely (Main Line) with the 9.10 a.m. Manchester (London Road) to Swansea in June 1959. This train, hauled from Manchester to Pontypool Road by a Longsight 'Royal Scot', 'Jubilee' or 'Patriot', was worked between Pontypool Road and Cardiff General by a Pontypool Road 'Grange', which then returned with the 4.40 p.m. Cardiff to Manchester as far as Hereford. At Cardiff, the train formation was reduced to 5 or 6 coaches for Swansea, though additional vehicles were attached on this occasion. The wagons in Ely Paper Mills (seen on the right) were probably ready to start the 4.20 p.m. through train to Woodford (ER) via Banbury, worked by a Canton 'WD' 2–8–0. The bridge in the background carried the ex-Taff Vale line from Penarth Curve to Radyr, which climbed after the junction at Leckwith Jct. South and crossed over the main line to the east of Ely station.

Llanelly 'Hall' No. 4941 *Llangedwyn Hall* passing through Ely (Main Line) station with a down freight on 3rd October 1957. The A48 road bridge is hidden behind the exhaust. This class 'H' goods was probably bound for Swansea or Llandilo Jct., and was formed with empty mineral and bolster wagons, both of which were common sights in South Wales up to the very end of steam, and beyond. 'Halls' were a common sight on the class 'C' and 'D' freights in and out of Llandilo Jct. at this time, with mostly '43s' and eight-coupled designs on slower, heavier trains, though the 5.50 pm. (class 'H') from Severn Tunnel Jct. to Llandilo Jct. was scheduled for a 'Hall' at this time.

Ely Main Line station on Monday, 25th May 1959, with the 12.45 p.m. Clarence Road to Pontypridd auto standing at the down platform behind Abercynon '6400' class 0–6–0PT No. 6435. At this time, the auto service comprised one morning and one afternoon return trip from Pontypridd to Cardiff, via St. Fagans. The bridge at the east end of the station (from which several earlier views were taken) carries the A48 Cardiff to Swansea road, whilst Ely paper mills may be seen beyond, on the right. The main station facilities were located on the up platform, with access only provided on the down.

MICHAEL HALE

Old Oak Common 'Castle' No. 5040 *Stokesay Castle* entering the west end of Ely (Main Line) station with the 11.10 a.m. Milford Haven to Paddington (No. 740) on Thursday, 3rd October 1957. Due into Paddington at 5.50 p.m., the train was formed of portions from Swansea (at the head, including the dining car), followed by three-coach sections from Milford Haven and Pembroke Dock. A coal merchant can be seen unloading a wagon in the mileage yard on the left. The goods siding passed around the back of the down platform, and rejoined the up main line by a trailing connection at the east end of the station. Ely (Main Line) signal box can be seen behind the engine, and visible beyond is part of the Crosswells Ales Brewery.

The former streamlined 'Castle' No. 5005 *Manorbier Castle* – at this time allocated to Cardiff (Canton), making a sequentially-numbered trio at the shed with No. 5006 *Tregenna Castle* and 5007 *Rougement Castle* – is seen here gathering speed through Ely with the 9.15 a.m. Manchester (London Road) to Swansea, which left Cardiff General at 2.28 p.m., on Monday, 10th October 1955. The morning Manchester train on Mondays (as well as Fridays and Saturdays) comprised the regular five-coach set with an additional Second, as seen here, but during the summer months it carried two extra coaches on those days to accommodate the heavier weekend traffic. The mileage siding had recently received house coal for coal merchants, one of whom, can be seen working a wagon at the far end.

S. RICKARD

Taken from a public footbridge at the west end of the mileage yard, this picture shows the 11.55 a.m. Paddington to Pembroke Dock and Milford Haven accelerating through Ely on Thursday, 3rd October 1957 behind Old Oak Common 'Castle' No. 5007 *Rougemont Castle*, a Canton engine from 1940 until the end of 1956. The wagons of coke standing in the up refuge siding were either for the brewery behind, or the paper mills. The protecting catch point for the mileage siding is clearly visible in the foreground, just inside the west end connection into the yard trailing out of the down main.

Coke trains often had the unusual appearance of high-sided wagons dotted through an otherwise uniform-height train, as with the 13th wagon on this train where the original wooden wagon had been built up to take a larger load of the light coke traffic. This picture shows Tondu's No. 5208 with an up class 'J' train of coke heading towards Ely station with three wagons of coal at the front, which had doubtless originated from Llantrisant yard with traffic from Cwm and Coedely coke ovens, and was bound for Guest Keens Steelworks on Cardiff Docks, on 10th October 1955. The engine would probably have worked the train into Pengam Sidings, from where dock trip services would have taken the wagons into the plant.

S. RICKARD

Swansea East Dock 2–8–0T No. 5232 approaching Ely station, with another up train of coke, this time originating in the Swansea area, and again probably bound for Guest Keens on Cardiff Docks on 15th June 1953. Some of the wagons towards the rear had the built-up sides, aimed at increasing the load from 6 to 10 tons of coke.

S. RICKARD

The up 'Pembroke Coast Express' seen during the early days of its existence, in the charge of Old Oak Common 'Hall' No. 5941 *Campion Hall*, a step or two down from the usual resplendent Landore 'Castle' that worked this prestigious train. The formation carried echoes of the past in the form of a number of ex-GWR coaches rather than a standard rake of chocolate-and-cream Mark I vehicles that soon became associated with this service. The leading four were the Swansea vehicles (including dining coaches), with the six Pembroke vehicles forming the rear portion. The train is seen approaching Ely station on Monday, 15th June 1953, a week after the commencement of the summer timetable in which the new, daily 10.55 a.m. Paddington and 1.0 p.m. Pembroke Dock service was introduced.

S. RICKARD

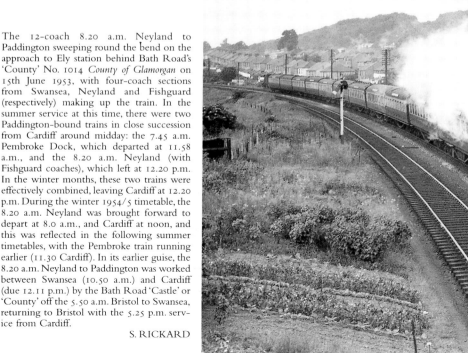

The 12-coach 8.20 a.m. Neyland to Paddington sweeping round the bend on the approach to Ely station behind Bath Road's 'County' No. 1014 *County of Glamorgan* on 15th June 1953, with four-coach sections from Swansea, Neyland and Fishguard (respectively) making up the train. In the summer service at this time, there were two Paddington-bound trains in close succession from Cardiff around midday: the 7.45 a.m. Pembroke Dock, which departed at 11.58 a.m., and the 8.20 a.m. Neyland (with Fishguard coaches), which left at 12.20 p.m. In the winter months, these two trains were effectively combined, leaving Cardiff at 12.20 p.m. During the winter 1954/5 timetable, the 8.20 a.m. Neyland was brought forward to depart at 8.0 a.m., and Cardiff at noon, and this was reflected in the following summer timetables, with the Pembroke train running earlier (11.30 Cardiff). In its earlier guise, the 8.20 a.m. Neyland to Paddington was worked between Swansea (10.50 a.m.) and Cardiff (due 12.11 p.m.) by the Bath Road 'Castle' or 'County' off the 5.50 a.m. Bristol to Swansea, returning to Bristol with the 5.25 p.m. service from Cardiff.

S. RICKARD

The same location but a more prestigious train: the inaugural run of the up 'South Wales Pullman', 4.35 p.m. Swansea to Paddington, running behind Landore 'Castle' No. 5013 *Abergavenny Castle*, highlighted by the evening sun on Monday, 27th June 1955. The 8-coach train worked down from Paddington at 8.50 a.m., immediately preceding the 8.55 a.m. through train to West Wales, but the operation of the service from the London end did not produce the anticipated results, and in 1961 the whole working was switched around to start from Swansea at 6.40 a.m., with a dramatic improvement in the up loading, though the return trip at 4.55 p.m. was still not so successful.
S. RICKARD

Rugby internationals at Cardiff Arms Park always brought a large number of special services from the Swansea area, stretching from Neath to Carmarthen, often starting in the Valleys. Here, Landore 'Hall' No. 6918 *Sandon Hall* was heading special No. 017 conveying Welsh supporters for the Wales v Scotland international on Saturday, 20th February 1954, in the days when Wales were nigh-on invincible to the home sides, particularly at home. How times have changed!
S. RICKARD

Evenings saw a succession of Class 'C' fast freight, milk and fish services heading east through the Cardiff area. Here, on 12th June 1957, the photographer had used the angle of the setting sun to help him go 'wrong side' to obtain this unusual view of Llanelly 'Grange' No. 6818 *Hardwick Grange* heading what may have been a tinplate train from Llandilo Jct., through Ely. The nearest track was the up refuge siding, on which coal traffic for Ely Brewery was placed, this siding remaining until the introduction of MAS.

S. RICKARD

Over the short distance between the outskirts of Ely and St. Fagans station, the line was bordered by attractive woodland on both sides. This picture shows Severn Tunnel's '42XX' 2–8–0 No. 5260 threading through the shadows with a down class 'H' freight on Thursday, 3rd October 1957. The leading wagons appear to have been carrying scrap metal, a common load in South Wales.

Leaving the woodland area behind, Old Oak Common 'Castle' No. 7025 *Sudeley Castle* is seen heading the down 'Pembroke Coast Express', 10.55 a.m. Paddington to Pembroke Dock, on the approach to St. Fagans station on Thursday, 3rd October 1957. A four-coach section for Pembroke was positioned at the head, and four for Swansea (including a leading dining car) at the rear. On summer Saturdays, the Pembroke portion was increased to eight or more vehicles, and positioned at the rear.

Taken from the end of St. Fagans down platform, this picture shows No. 48738, from Shrewsbury shed, heading a down class 'H' freight past an indicator showing the start or end of a temporary speed restriction, on 4th November 1955. The use of LMS '8F' 2–8–0s on the South Wales main line stretched back to the autumn of 1940, when a number were loaned to the Great Western for a short period. They became quite common again in the latter part of the Second World War with the building of eighty at Swindon during 1943–5 (Nos. 8400–79), these being sent to the LMS in 1946/7.

ST. FAGANS

The main line passenger and freight services through St. Fagans were punctuated periodically by the Cardiff (Clarence Road) and Pontypridd auto service, powered by an Abercynon '64XX' carrying target JB. Here, the 1.39 p.m. Pontypridd was leaving St. Fagans for Cardiff on 3rd October 1957, propelled by No. 6438, which, with No. 6411, were the two engines normally employed at this time. The train ran between Pontypridd and Tynycaeau Jct. over the former Barry Railway's Trehafod to Cadoxton main line. Following the closure of the Barry Railway station at Pontypridd (Graig), these trains crossed to the ex-TaffVale route at Treforest Junction to use the TV station at Pontypridd. Leaving the Barry route at Tynycaeau Junction, the train then took the single line down to join the main line at St. Fagans, where the Barry Railway formerly had exchange sidings and a goods shed. By the time of this photograph, the branch service via St. Fagans had been reduced to two down (from Pontypridd) and two up auto trains daily, although an additional trip from Creigiau (ex-Cadoxton) to Clarence Road was carried out by another car. Between each of its arrivals at and departures from Cardiff, the Abercynon unit was employed on Clarence Road and Penarth trips.

Between Ely and St. Fagans stations, the South Wales Main Line passes through some lovely woodland areas, the accompanying main road being on a high level with banks shelving down to the line, south of which the River Ely meanders, crossed four times by the railway. St. Fagans itself was the epitome of an attractive country station, with station house at the east end of the up platform, a substantial river bridge over the River Ely at the west end of the platforms, along with a level crossing, the station signal box and junction with the former Barry Railway. The station had up and down platforms with a cattle pen alongside the up platform, taken out of use in 1959, whilst the station itself closed in 1962.

The Station signal box dated from 1889, when the Barry Railway opened the connecting line from their Trehafod & Cadoxton main line at Tynycaeau Junction down to St. Fagans for mineral and goods traffic, and passenger trains from Pontypridd (Graig) to Cardiff (Clarence Road). The Barry Railway line into St. Fagans opened on 13th May 1889, and was double line with three exchange sidings. They also had their own goods shed, and a signal box located on the north side of their running lines, midway along the sidings. The Earl of Plymouth (Chairman of the Barry Railway Company), who resided at St. Fagans Castle, had his own private halt, located at the east end of the Barry's line (level with the GWR section between the Station box and the junction with the Barry's line.)

November 1914 saw the GWR make several additions to the operational layout at St. Fagans, such was the level of activity there. A down goods loop was provided approximately 40 chains (½ mile) long, and a new signal box at St. Fagans West opened, controlling exit from the down loop and also the connections between the main line and the west end of the Barry's sidings. The new box replaced the former West box (located adjacent to the western junction with the Barry's sidings), which had opened in 1889. The new St. Fagans West Box closed in December 1935, when the down loop was shortened by 16 chains at its western end.

With the closure of the station on 10th September 1962, the former Barry line was also closed to traffic, being used only by the Pontypridd to Clarence Road service which had changed from a steam-hauled auto service to a 2-car DMU in September 1960. It was, however, retained as a diversionary route for trains from and to the Rhymney Valley when Caerphilly Tunnel was closed for engineering work, and would also still have been used for Royal Trains en route to Wenvoe Tunnel for

The 6.0 p.m. Saturdays-only Cardiff to Bridgend stopper drawing into St. Fagans behind Landore 'Hall' No. 6918 *Sandon Hall* on 20th June 1959. Allocated to Landore in June 1941, No. 6918 remained there until June1961, and had undergone the silver buffer treatment which distinguished Landore engines at this time. The five-coach corridor set in use on this train was running a circuit that started on Saturdays with the 7.15 a.m. Cardiff to Birmingham and the 11.40 a.m. return, and following the 6.0 p.m. Cardiff, empty stock from Bridgend to Swansea. Two different designs of lamp can be seen on the platforms.

Taken shortly before all the Canton 'Britannias' were transferred to the London Midland Region, this pictures shows a high-mileage No. 70025 *Western Star* passing through St. Fagans with the 10.35 a.m. Kensington to Whitland milk empties, which it had taken over outside Canton shed (4.57–5.45 p.m.), on 30th August 1961. The train comprises eight or so tanks with a passenger brake on the rear, and would call at Felin Fran for train crew purposes, then at Llanelly and Carmarthen en route to Whitland.

The Up South Wales Pullman (4.30 p.m. Swansea to Paddington) sweeping through St. Fagans behind Landore Castle No. 5006 *Tregenna Castle*, in this view taken from the station footbridge on Wednesday, 30th August 1961. Accommodation comprised First and Second class parlour and kitchen cars, with brake Seconds at the outer ends. Meals or refreshments were served at every seat, and a 10s 0d (First class) or 5s 0d (Second) supplement was payable on a single journey between the two cities, with a diminishing scale from Neath, Port Talbot, Bridgend, Cardiff, and Newport (7s 0d and 4s 0d). The access to the former cattle pens can be seen behind the up platform, with the trackwork and connection removed by this stage.

Deputising for the normal Landore 'Castle', Canton 'Hall' No. 4953 *Pitchford Hall* is seen running through St. Fagans station on 20th June 1959 with the down 'Capitals United Express', 3.55 p.m. Paddington to Fishguard Harbour. During the summer timetable, when the 3.45 p.m. boat service from Paddington to Fishguard ran in addition to the 3.55 p.m., the Canton engine off the up 'Red Dragon' returned with the 3.45 p.m., while the 3.55 p.m. was worked by a Landore 'Castle' off the previous night's 9.35 p.m. Swansea (6.50 p.m. Neyland) to Paddington. Doubtless to maximize its popularity, the 'Capitals United' was advertised in the leading 'green pages' of the public timetables showing Paddington and Cardiff times only, with, unusually, no mention of the intermediate calls at Badminton or Newport, or those to the west of Cardiff. However, all was made abundantly clear within the body of those timetables! Despite the disintegrating siding alongside, the station platforms at this model of a country station were in a well-kept condition.

A view from the station footbridge, with the attractive countryside on the north side of the line sloping down to the Ely River, which itself has crossed under the line four times within the final mile to St. Fagans. '72XX' 2–8–2T No. 7207 of Landore is seen entering the station with a down mixed class 'H' freight on 4th November 1955, with possibly scrap materials being carried by the opens in the centre of the train. The buildings on this platform were raised off the ground, doubtless to minimise damage should the adjacent Ely River (now joined into one channel) flood. The cattle pens on the left were served by a short spur leading off the up main at the east end of the station.

overnight stabling, as and when required. However, on 30th March 1963, Tynycaeau Junction signal box burnt down and all movements over the line ceased.

The introduction of MAS saw St. Fagans box reduced to a ground frame to control the level crossing, the down goods loop being taken out of use, and all the connections with the former Barry line recovered, leaving plain track, but with a crossover from the down line to the up. In May 1966, the ground frame was transferred to the down side, but in June 1986, it was moved back to a new box on the site of the original signal box on the up side, and was upgraded to control also the crossings at St. George's and Llantrisant West, a position which remains current. All crossings are double barrier with closed-circuit TV, the control panel being at St. Fagans. The crossover from the down to up main was removed as part of the 1966 modifications.

Trains meeting at St. Fagans. The 3.55 p.m. Paddington to Fishguard Harbour, hauled by a Landore 'Castle', passing the eastbound 3.50 p.m. Milford Haven to Weymouth fish train behind a Canton 'Hall', running early, as the two were due to pass around Bridgend. This view, looking west from the station footbridge, emphasizes the compactness of the west end of the station, where the station building, river bridge, level crossing and signal box, all squeezed into an area of around a hundred yards.

The way west through St. Fagans, showing the station building in the right foreground, the level crossing (carrying the road from St. Fagans village, to the right, to Michaelston and the A48) and the adjacent signal box. A trailing crossover between the main lines was provided next to the signal box, with a double junction to the branch to Tynycaeau Junction diverging to the right just beyond it, and the down loop in the distance. The track curved first to the left, as seen in the distance, and then to the right under the former Barry Railway viaduct. Canton 'Britannia' No. 70029 *Shooting Star* was heading the 3.55 p.m. Paddington to Fishguard Harbour, leaning to the curve through the station, c. 1955.

A classic Canton turnout for a top-link 'Britannia'. No. 70024 *Vulcan* heading across the river bridge through St. Fagans with the 1.55 p.m. Paddington to Neyland and Pembroke Dock (No. 169) on Monday, 1st July 1957. For the engine, this was the return working of the 8.0 a.m. Cardiff to Paddington (6.30 a.m. Swansea), and the engine would return from Swansea that night with the 9.10 p.m. service to Cardiff. As the engine turned at Ranelagh Bridge, no coal could be taken after leaving Canton shed until reaching Landore, and skilful firing was necessary to ensure the coal supply held out to Swansea.

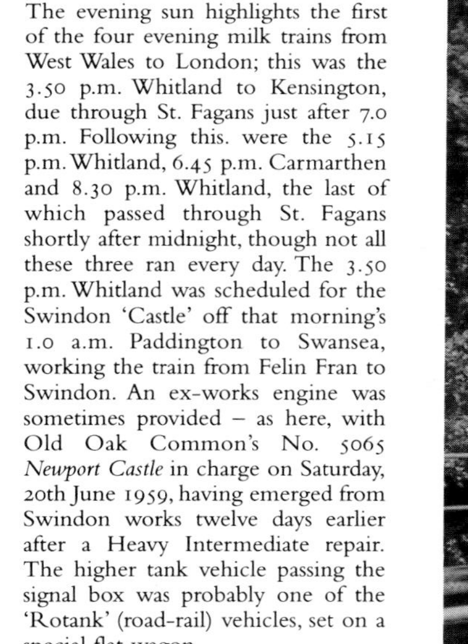

The evening sun highlights the first of the four evening milk trains from West Wales to London; this was the 3.50 p.m. Whitland to Kensington, due through St. Fagans just after 7.0 p.m. Following this. were the 5.15 p.m. Whitland, 6.45 p.m. Carmarthen and 8.30 p.m. Whitland, the last of which passed through St. Fagans shortly after midnight, though not all these three ran every day. The 3.50 p.m. Whitland was scheduled for the Swindon 'Castle' off that morning's 1.0 a.m. Paddington to Swansea, working the train from Felin Fran to Swindon. An ex-works engine was sometimes provided – as here, with Old Oak Common's No. 5065 *Newport Castle* in charge on Saturday, 20th June 1959, having emerged from Swindon works twelve days earlier after a Heavy Intermediate repair. The higher tank vehicle passing the signal box was probably one of the 'Rotank' (road-rail) vehicles, set on a special flat wagon.

The view from the station footbridge, looking west, with Canton's Modified 'Hall' No. 6969 *Wraysbury Hall* – on one of the depot's '75XXX' ('Class 4') turns – running over the level crossing and into the station with the four-coach 10.15 a.m. Carmarthen to Cheltenham train on Thursday, 3rd October 1957. Earlier that morning, the engine had worked west on the 7.35 a.m. Chepstow to Swansea, and after working the Cheltenham train as far as Gloucester, would return from there with the 3.40 p.m. to Cardiff. The coach programme indicated that the set shown started its day at Swansea, and would finish it around 7.0 pm. at Swindon, whilst the van forming tail traffic was probably a milk churn vehicle destined for Cardiff or Treherbert.

This view, taken from the bank of the River Ely on the afternoon of 4th November 1955, shows Llanelly '28XX' 2–8–0 No. 3851 crossing the river bridge at the west end of St. Fagans station with a down 'F' class freight. This train was probably the 1.15 p.m. Severn Tunnel Jct. to Llandilo Jct., which was due to pass through St. Fagans at about 2.15 p.m. Having split into two channels near St. Fagans viaduct, a half-mile to the west, the Ely River became one again at this point.

An early 1950s view of the 8.10 am. Swansea to York service (via the Great Central route) crossing the Ely River bridge at St. Fagans behind Landore 'Castle' No. 7003 *Elmley Castle*, which would work the train to Banbury, and return with the balancing service. The origin of this train was the 'Ports-to-Ports' express from Barry to Newcastle via Gloucester and the Banbury & Cheltenham line, introduced in 1906, and provided to convey sea-faring personnel, passengers and other trades between the several ports on the route. This service was extended westwards to Swansea in 1920, though still running via Barry and the Vale of Glamorgan. There was also a through coach to and from Hull. In the postwar era, the train was rerouted via the Severn Tunnel, Swindon and Oxford, and mostly truncated back to York, though one train per week in each direction at this time was extended through to Newcastle once more. It also took to the main line between Cardiff and Bridgend rather than running via Barry, as the 'seafaring' aspect of the train had diminished greatly. The stock was provided by the Great Western and the Great Central (later L & NE) companies, and this train still comprised Gresley vehicles. During the 1930s, the train was worked in both directions by Banbury '43XXs', and for a few months before the Second World War by their new 'Manors'. J. G. HUBBACK

An atmospheric view of St. Fagans on a sunny, late autumnal afternoon, 4th November 1955, with the westbound 11.55 a.m. Paddington to West Wales (Swansea and Milford Haven) service, train No. 167, crossing the river bridge over the River Ely behind Old Oak Common Castle No. 7004 *Eastnor Castle*. The bracket signal shows the centre signal off for the down main line, the left-hand signal (as viewed) controlling the connection across to the former Barry Railway line to Tynycaeau, and the right-hand signal the down goods loop.

Landore 2–8–2T No. 7200 (now preserved) accelerating away to the west of St. Fagans station, with a down class 'H' freight during the evening of Saturday, 20th June 1959. The engine is pictured opposite the junction with the former Barry Railway line to Pontypridd via Tynycaeau Junction. St. Fagans signal box can be clearly seen on the up side, and there was a temporary speed restriction in operation on the up main, denoted by the indicator board showing 'C' for commencement of restriction.

The 7.10 pm. Cardiff to Swansea parcels on the down main, west of St. Fagans station, behind Llanelly Mogul No. 6310 on 20th June1959. As with many local parcels services, these trains frequently conveyed vans off long-distance services, as was probably the case with the ex-LNE vehicle behind the tender.

St. Fagans was an excellent place to observe main-line freight traffic at speed, yet still offered the chance to appreciate the detail of the train's composition. Here '72xx' 2–8–2T No. 7225 was nearing the signal box on the up main with an 'H' class freight on 3rd October 1957, with the watering pipe and the driver's leg casually hanging from the cab. With the exception of the three oil tanks near the head, the train comprised open and mineral wagons, the majority of which were wooden designs. St. Fagans viaduct may be seen in the distance.

This photograph from St. Fagans signal box, shows Landore 'Castle' No. 7021 *Haverfordwest Castle* heading west with the 3.45 p.m. Paddington to Fishguard Harbour on 30th August 1961. The earlier pointwork arrangements near the signal box were changed in 1957; the trailing crossover between the mains at the west end of the box was removed, whilst the former double junction between the mains and the Tynycaeau line was replaced by a facing crossover from the down to up main and a trailing point on the up main for access to and from the branch, which was singled onwards. The entry into the down loop is seen beyond the engine.

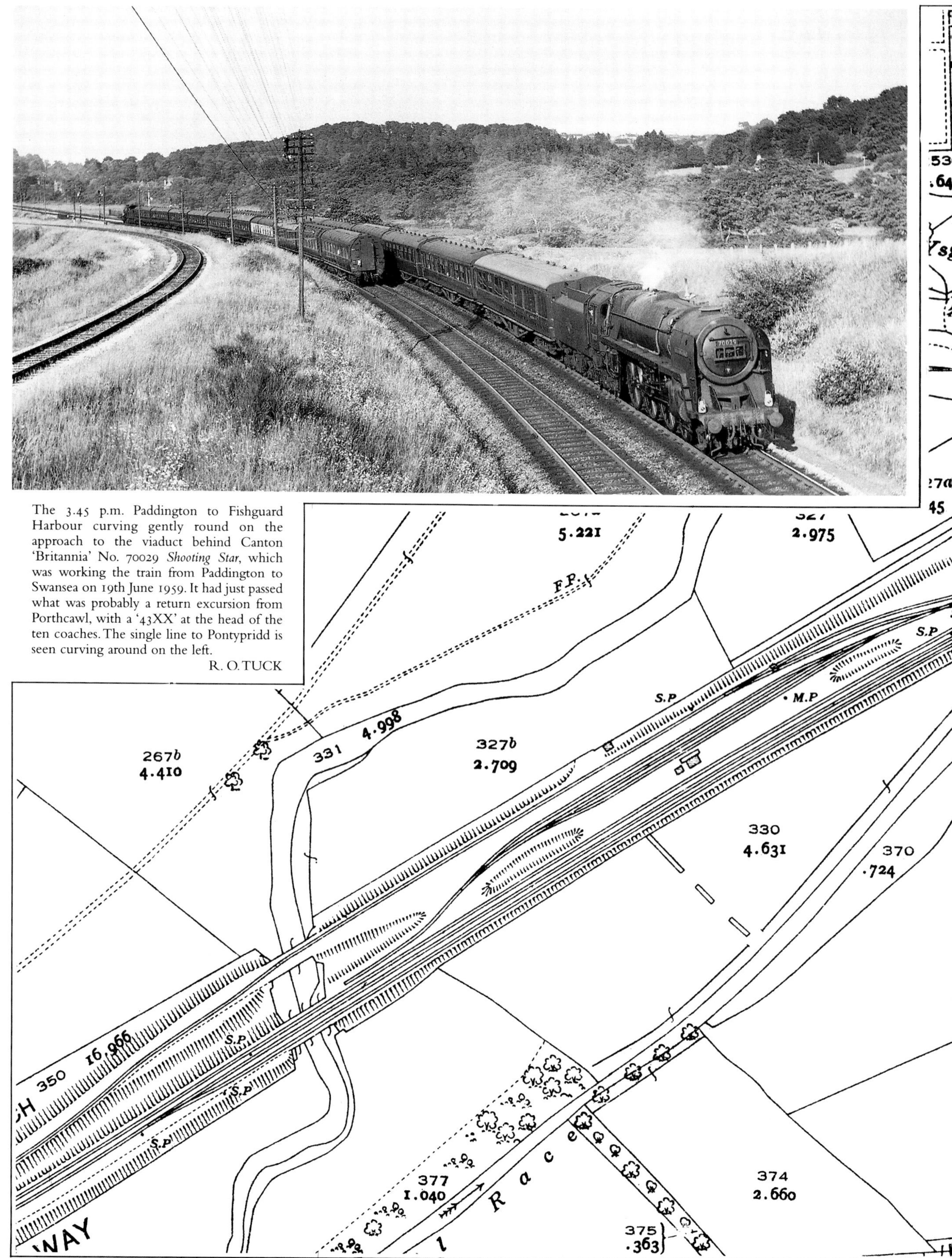

The 3.45 p.m. Paddington to Fishguard Harbour curving gently round on the approach to the viaduct behind Canton 'Britannia' No. 70029 *Shooting Star*, which was working the train from Paddington to Swansea on 19th June 1959. It had just passed what was probably a return excursion from Porthcawl, with a '43XX' at the head of the ten coaches. The single line to Pontypridd is seen curving around on the left.

R. O. TUCK

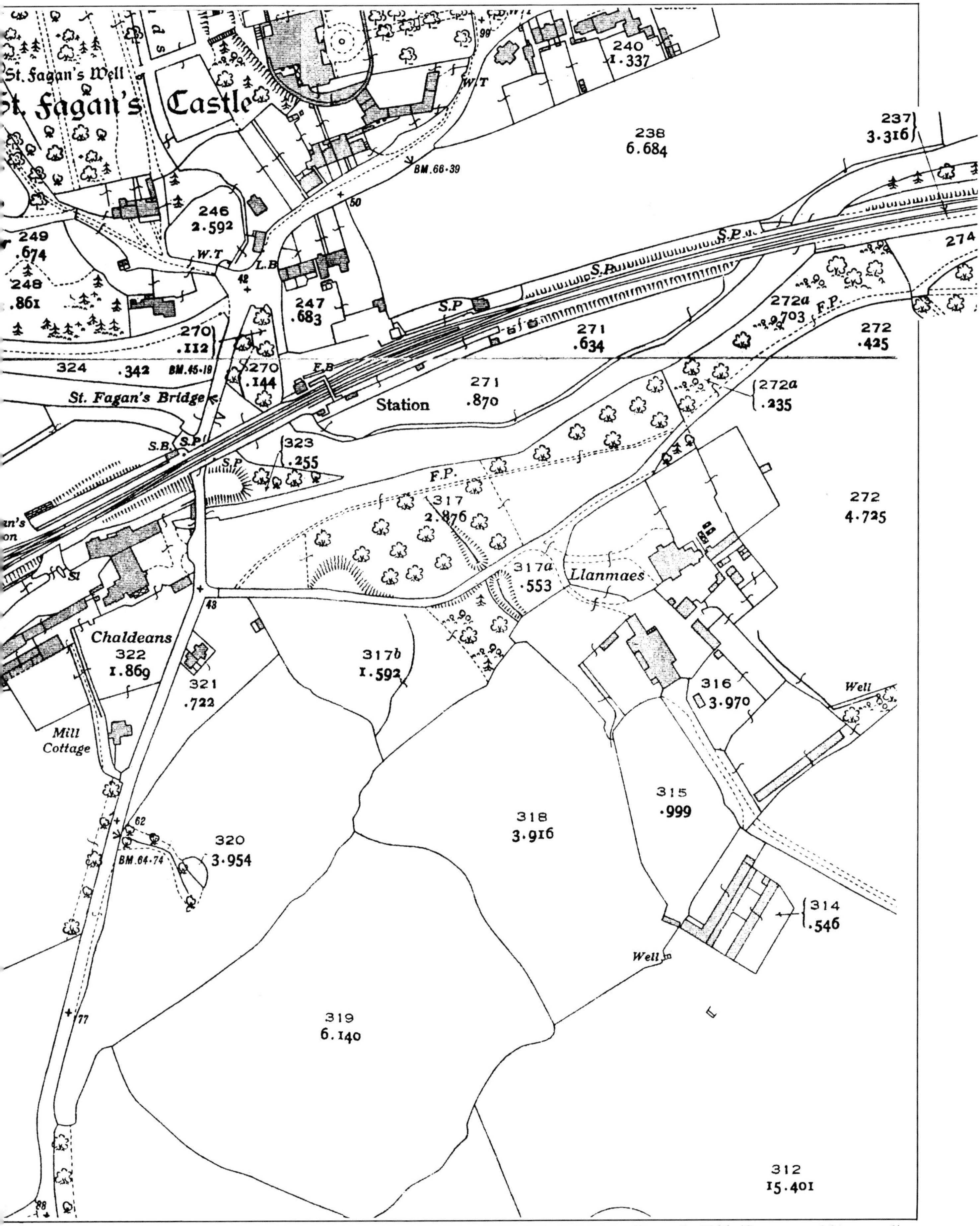

Taken from 25-inch Ordnance Survey for 1936. (Crown copyright reserved)

ST. FAGANS VIADUCT

In the late September sun this picture shows Landore 'Castle' No. 5077 *Fairey Battle* heading the five-coach 9.10 a.m. Manchester (London Road) to Swansea around to the viaduct on 29th September 1956. An LMR brake van was conveyed at the back of the through portion from Manchester, whilst at Shrewsbury, two coaches from Birkenhead were added to the rear, all three being detached at Cardiff. R. O. TUCK

Canton turn 'H17', the 2.40 p.m. Cardiff (Penarth Curve) to Tondu class 'K' mixed goods, heading along the down main west of St. Fagans behind Canton's 0–6–2T No. 5633 on Saturday, 29th September 1956. The load included pipework, metal railing and coal.
R. O. TUCK

After St. Fagans, the line curved slightly towards the south, then gently back to the west as the down loop was left behind. Here, ex-works Landore 'Castle' No. 5013 *Abergavenny Castle*, in typically pristine condition, is seen approaching the Barry Railway viaduct with the 8.55 a.m. Paddington to Pembroke Dock service on 28th February 1959. During the winter months, this train normally conveyed a three-coach section for Pembroke Dock and a pair for Neyland at the front, with a four-coach section (including a dining car) for Swansea at the rear, though one or two strengthening vehicles were sometimes added. The single line on a rising gradient in the centre left was the former Barry Railway line to Pontypridd. R. O. TUCK

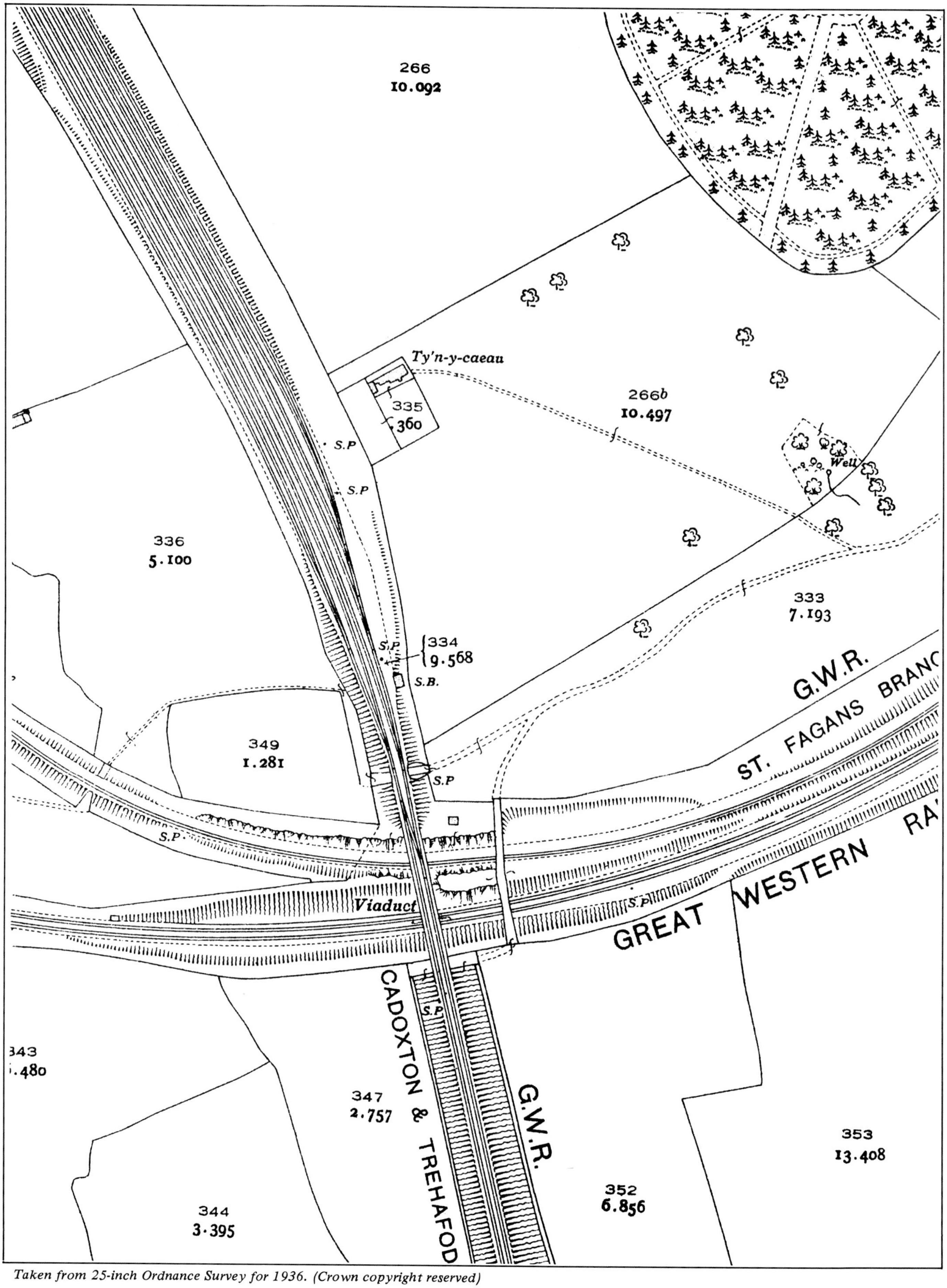

266
10.092

Ty'n-y-caeau

335
.360

266b
10.497

Well

S.P

S.P

336
5.100

333
7.193

S.P
334
9.568

S.B.

G.W.R.
ST. FAGANS BRANC

349
1.281

S.P

S.P

GREAT WESTERN RA

Viaduct

S.P

S.P

CADOXTON & TREHAFOD

G.W.R.

343
.480

347
2.757

353
13.408

352
6.856

344
3.395

Taken from 25-inch Ordnance Survey for 1936. (Crown copyright reserved)

Abercynon's No. 6438 taking the former Barry Railway line from St. Fagans to Tynycaeau Junction, with the 12.45 p.m. Cardiff (Clarence Road) to Pontypridd auto service ('JB') on Saturday, 28th February 1959. This 14-mile journey to Pontypridd was a couple of miles longer than the direct ex-Taff Vale route, and took around five minutes more. This loop was originally double track, but was singled in 1934. R. O. TUCK

The 180-yard ex-Barry Railway viaduct carrying its line from Cadoxton to Trehafod is clearly shown in the background of this picture of Old Oak Common 'Castle' No. 7036 *Taunton Castle* passing underneath and around the curve at the head of the 11.10 a.m. Milford Haven to Paddington on Saturday, 29th September 1956. The viaduct (at 175m 01c) towered above a rather lower occupation bridge in the foreground that, like the viaduct, spanned both the main lines and the ex-Barry line to Tynycaeau Junction; it was demolished in October 1981. R. O. TUCK

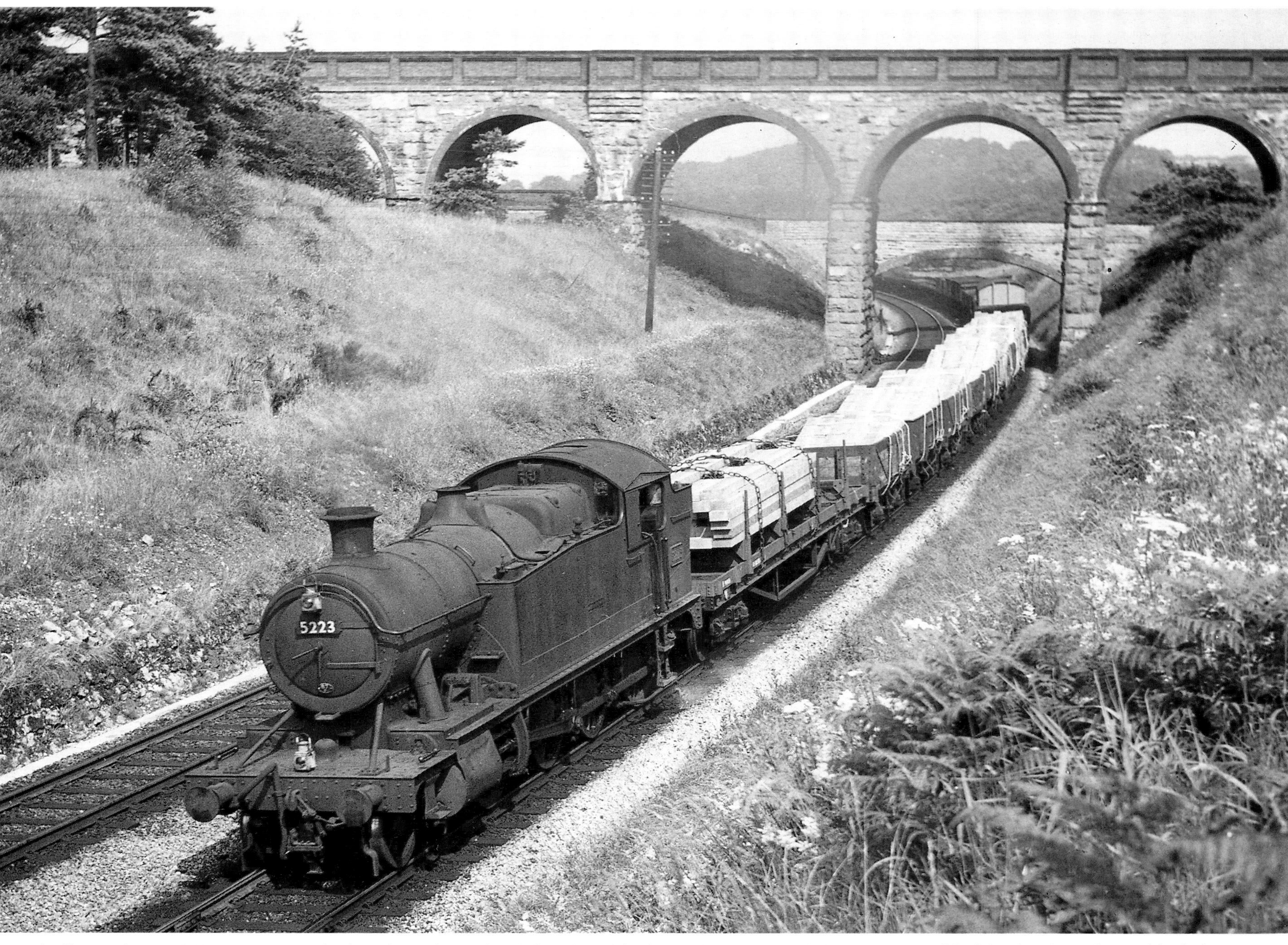

Llanelly 4200 class 2–8–0T No. 5223 passing under the viaduct with a westbound class 'H' mixed freight on 16th July 1955. The leading wagons were all loaded with timber, with general freight forming the rest of the train, which was probably bound for Llandilo Jct. There was a considerable amount of timber conveyed to the pits in South Wales during the heyday of the coal industry. J. G. HUBBACK

Heading a down express on 17th March 1956, was Landore 'Castle' No. 5041 *Tiverton Castle* seen passing under the viaduct with a good head of white exhaust, no doubt produced from best Welsh steam coal. The first two coaches were of 1937 stock, with deep corridor windows. R. O. TUCK

The 1.55 p.m. Paddington to Pembroke Dock passing under the ex-Barry Railway viaduct west of St. Fagans on 19th June 1959. This was a scheduled Canton 'Britannia' turn from Paddington to Swansea, but is seen here hauled by Bristol Bath Road 'County' No. 1011 *County of Chester*, which had obviously been substituted, probably at Paddington, creating a rare event for this train. Other motive power on this service included a 'Hall' from Swansea, a '43XX' from Carmarthen, and a '45XX' from Whitland to Pembroke. The balancing service for the stock on this train was the 8.0 a.m. Neyland, pictured earlier, which was worked on alternate days. R. O. TUCK

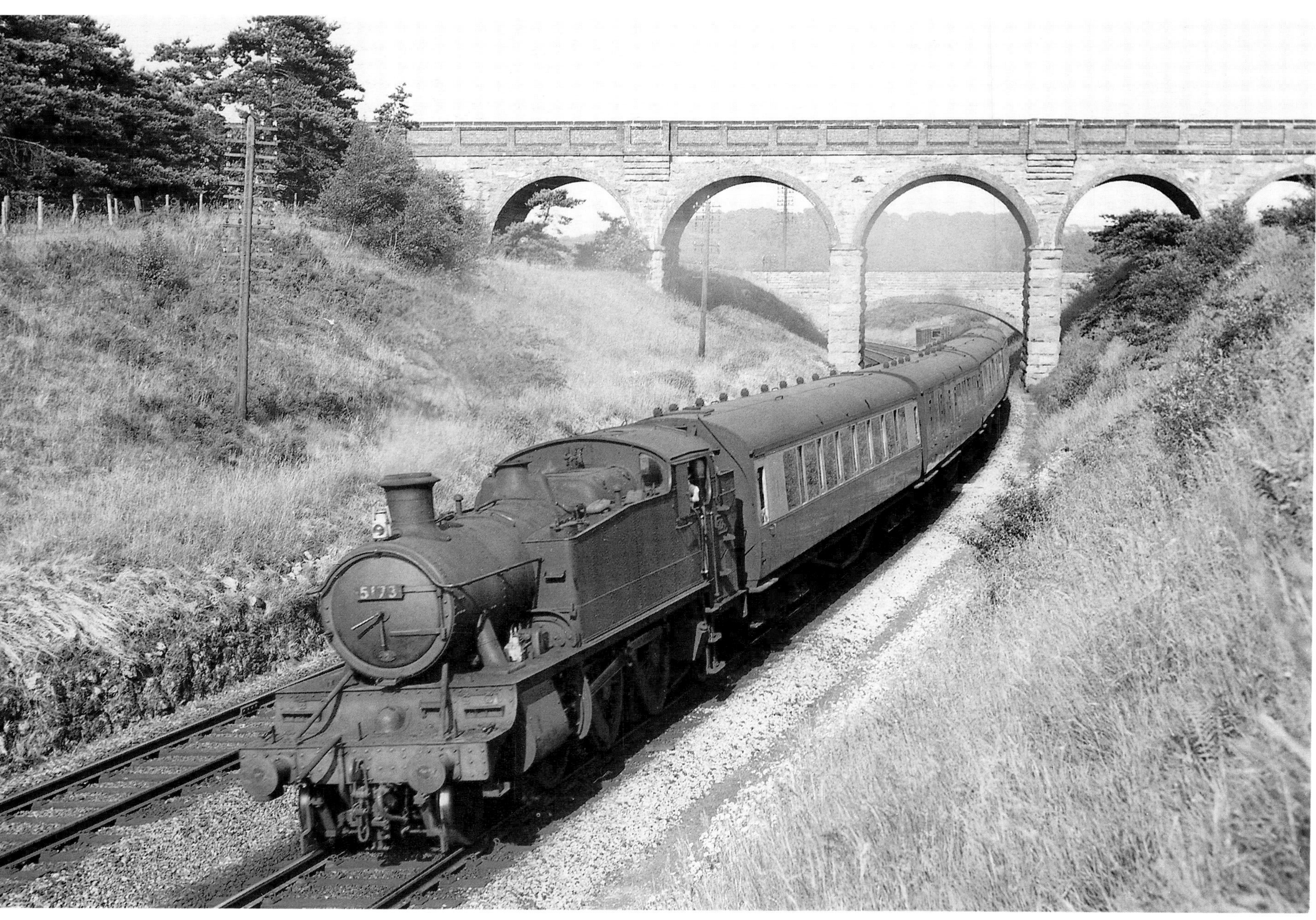

There were not many 2–6–2Ts to be seen on the section west of Cardiff, but one worked regularly on the 5.25 p.m. Cardiff to Porthcawl commuter train, here passing under the viaduct on Friday, 19th June 1959. The Ebbw Junction '51XX' prairie tank No. 5173 was scheduled to return with the coaches as the 6.50 p.m. Porthcawl to Newport, which in the summer was used by the many day-trippers to this seaside venue. The coach set was one of three 5-coach corridor rakes that worked in a cycle variously between Newport, Gloucester, Cheltenham, Cardiff, Porthcawl and Newport, and to Birmingham and back on Saturdays.

R. O. TUCK

ST. GEORGE'S

The impressive Barry Railway Viaduct, built in 1889 to carry their main line over the Great Western main line at 175m 01ch, ceased to carry traffic from the mid-1960s when the former Barry line was closed. It remained in situ for some 15 years but, as part of the construction of the westwards extension of the M4 Motorway beyond Cardiff, and a slip road from Culverhouse Cross, it was demolished in October 1981.

Beyond the viaduct the line curves north-west and sweeps around the hamlet of St. George's, running alongside the country road through the village. The level crossing at 175m 61ch was operated from a ground frame, the installation being modernised with FLBs in 1976. From June 1986, the ground frame was taken out of use and the barriers controlled from St. Fagans (qv).

Only a month after emerging from Swindon Works following a 'Heavy General' overhaul, Landore 'Castle' No. 5080 *Defiant* had been well turned-out for her run on the up 'South Wales Pullman', the 4.30 p.m. Swansea to Paddington. The train is seen here rounding the bend from St, George's for the run under the viaduct and through St. Fagans on Friday, 19th June 1959. Having already called at Neath, Port Talbot and Bridgend, the Pullman would stop at Cardiff and Newport on the way to Paddington, where it was due at 8.45 p.m. The Pullman service comprised a pair of Brake Seconds at the outer ends, with six First and Second class Parlour and Kitchen Cars between. R .O. TUCK

An early 1950s view with WD 2-8-0 No. 90693 rounding the bend from St. George's to St. Fagans viaduct, at the head of a lengthy up class 'H' goods service which probably started from Llandilo Junction or Swansea, bound for Severn Tunnel or beyond. The train contained a good mixture of freight wagons, with a 'Plate' and 'Tube' wagon, vans, tanks, sheeted opens and container wagons all included in the visible part. No. 90693 was stationed variously at St. Philip's Marsh, Llanelly and Neath in 1952, and Canton in 1955. J. G. HUBBACK

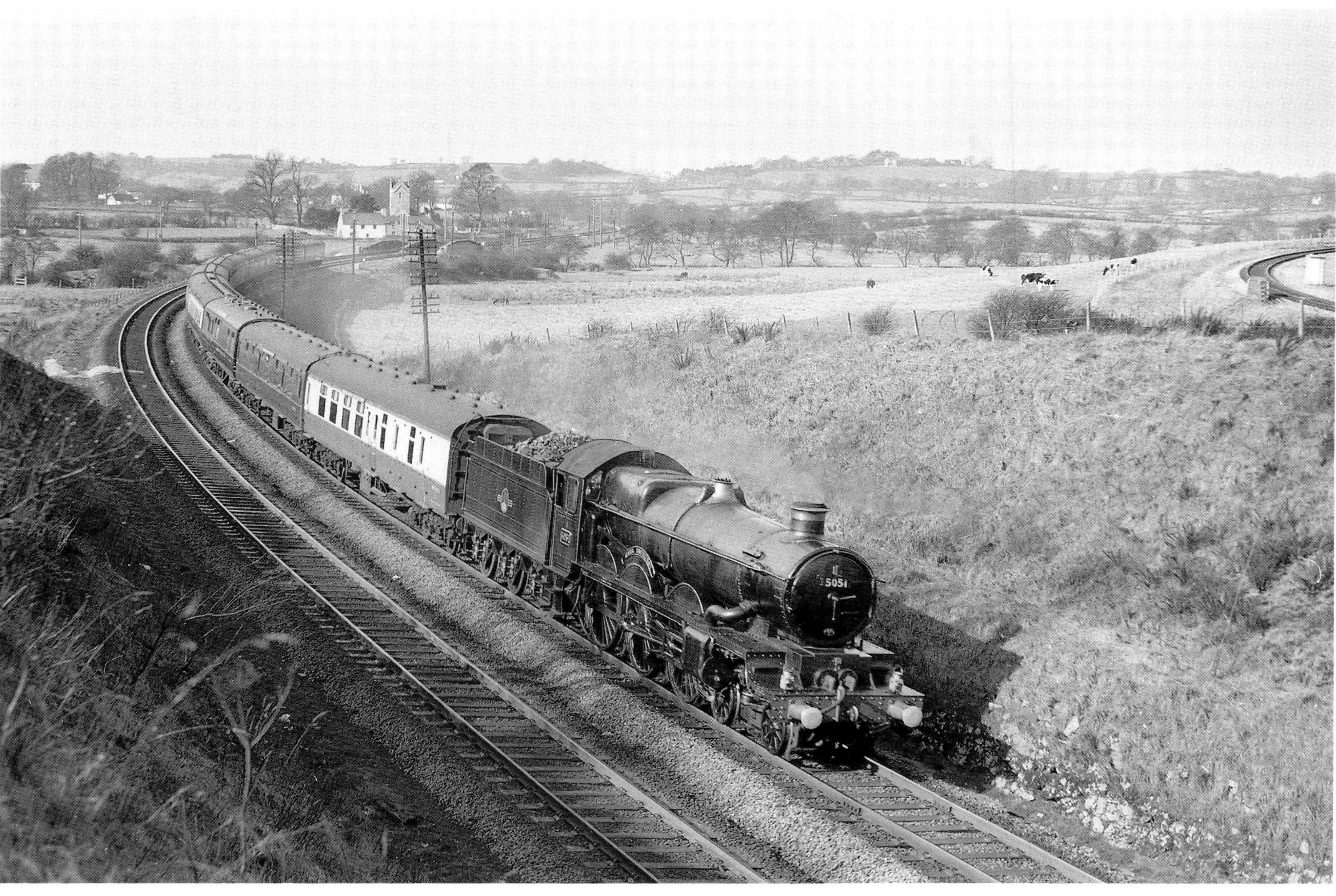

The picturesque nature of the line in the St. George's to St. Fagans area is nicely shown in this view of the 8.0 a.m. Neyland to Paddington service heading round the curve towards the former Barry Railway viaduct on Saturday, 29th February 1959. Due into Paddington at 3.10 p.m., the train conveyed coaches from Swansea (at the head including a twin dining set), Neyland, Fishguard Harbour and Pembroke Dock. The two trains (7.30 a.m. Pembroke and 8.0 a.m. Neyland) that had run separately throughout the week during the summer months were, like the winter train seen here, combined from summer 1959, except on Saturdays. Landore 'Castle' No. 5051 *Earl Bathurst* is seen in charge of the 8.0 a.m. Neyland service, which it would hand over at Cardiff to a Canton 'Britannia' for the run to Paddington. Earlier in its journey, the train was scheduled for Neyland 'County' haulage from Neyland to Carmarthen, then a Landore 'Castle' on to Swansea. R. O. TUCK

A half-mile or so west of the ex-Barry Railway viaduct is the village of St. George's (which in various 20th century sources was also named as St. George, and St. Georges-super-Ely). At St. George's, the line runs alongside the country road from the village to the church providing ready access to the lineside for photography. This view shows Ebbw Junction 'Grange' No. 6865 *Hopton Grange* passing on the up main with the 12.40 p.m. Carmarthen to Cheltenham (3.42 p.m. ex-Cardiff) on Thursday, 12th June 1958, running with tail traffic front and rear, still a common sight at this time. The coach programme identifies the leading vehicle as conveying fish from Milford Haven to Salisbury and Chichester, whilst the rear van was loaded with milk churns from Carmarthen to Cardiff.

92½ tons of Llanelly's '72XX' 2-8-2T No. 7228 rumbling past St. George's with a down class 'H' freight train on 15th June 1958, shaking the ground with the force of the momentum involved. Her train consisted largely of empty mineral wagons. Llanelly's heavy tank engines ran daily to Cardiff, Newport, Pontypool Road and Severn Tunnel Jct., often changing engines at Cardiff or Severn Tunnel Jct. on those trains destined for English yards.

A new duty taken by Canton in the 1958 summer service was the 8.48 a.m. Fishguard Harbour to Paddington parcels train, as between Landore (12.15 pm.) and Cardiff. The train was diagrammed for a Canton 'Castle' (MWF), alternating with a Neyland 'County' (TThS), but a high-mileage 'Britannia' would normally be used. Here, No. 70018 *Flying Dutchman* was heading the train through St. George's in June 1958. This train did not call at either Carmarthen or Swansea (High Street) stations, attaching empty vans at Carmarthen Junction off the 12.45 a.m. (News) Paddington to Carmarthen, and Enparts vans for Swindon Works at Landore. Vehicles for Kensington were also conveyed. At Cardiff, it would again pick up empty vans from the newspaper train. This service evolved from the original morning Fishguard Irish cattle and perishable trains of pre-First World War era, and received its distinctive '8.48' departure around 1938.

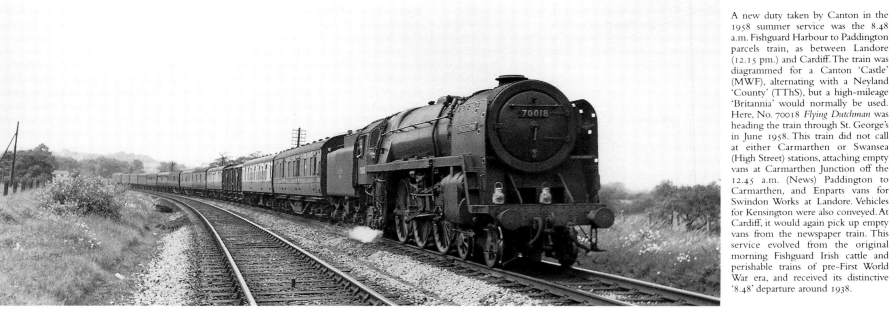

The class 'D' 12.5 p.m. Llandilo Junction to Cambridge freight, a Llanelly turn, was a fly-weight train as far as the Cardiff yards, where it picked up traffic for Oxford and East Anglia. This view shows the train passing St. George's on Thursday, 12th June 1958 behind Neyland Mogul No. 5324. At Canton, the engine would be changed for an Oxford locomotive, which ranged through 'Halls', Standard 'Class 4s' to high-mileage 'Castles'. The train was scheduled to call only at Margam en route to Cardiff and thereafter at Newport, Gloucester and (running via Honeybourne) Kingham on its way to Yarnton.

A study of Llanelly Mogul No. 7314 heading a down part-fitted class 'E' express freight through St. George's on the afternoon of Thursday, 12th June 1958. Cattle vans, seen at the head of the train, were an increasingly uncommon sight by this time.

Being run in by Canton after overhaul at Caerphilly Works, Old Oak Common's No. 5936 *Oakley Hall* is seen here running through St. George's with the 9. 10 a.m. Manchester (London Road) to Swansea on Monday, 16th June 1958. The train would call at Bridgend, Port Talbot and Neath, and was due into Swansea at 3.50 p.m. The engine returned from Swansea at 6.55 p.m. with the 5.18 p.m. Carmarthen to Bristol service as far as Cardiff.

From a photographic vantage point at track level, the sight of a 'Britannia' Pacific bearing down in full flight was awesome. In the summer of 1958, the 11.55 a.m. Paddington to West Wales service was worked by a Canton 'Britannia', though not off the 8.0 a.m. ex-Cardiff as the Canton LDC always pressed for. Here, No. 70016 *Ariel* is seen passing through St. George's at speed on Thursday, 12th June 1958, a few days into the summer timetable. The engine's handhold cut-outs in the smoke deflectors – which replaced earlier handrails – are clearly seen here.

A class '9' ('J') up freight, probably from Tondu or Llantrisant, heading along the up main through St. George's on Thursday, 14th February 1957, behind Tondu 2–8–0T No. 4276. The train largely comprised loaded mineral wagons, including wooden vehicles, though the latter were in significant decline by this time; it was probably conveying house coal from the Tondu Valley to station yards in the Cardiff and Newport areas.

Stanier '8F' 2–8–0 No. 48431 from St. Philip's Marsh shed bringing a down PW train of bogie bolsters past St. Georges on 12th June 1958. The '8Fs' were no strangers to the South Wales main line, as 25 had been loaned to the Great Western shortly after the outbreak of the Second World War, whilst a batch of 80 had been constructed at Swindon between 1943 and 1945, being used all over the system until 1946/7. No. 8431 was one of that batch, constructed at Swindon in March 1944 and based in the West Country and at Gloucester until transferred to the LMS in March 1947. She re-appeared on the Western Region in the latter 1950s.

PETERSTON

The eastern approaches to Peterston, showing the former Barry Railway sidings on the right, taken on 5th August 1963; from the far end of the sidings, a connecting line ran to Drope Junction, on the Pontypridd & Cadoxton line to the south of St. Fagans viaduct. There were seven roads in the yard, of which three were dead-end. MICHAEL HALE

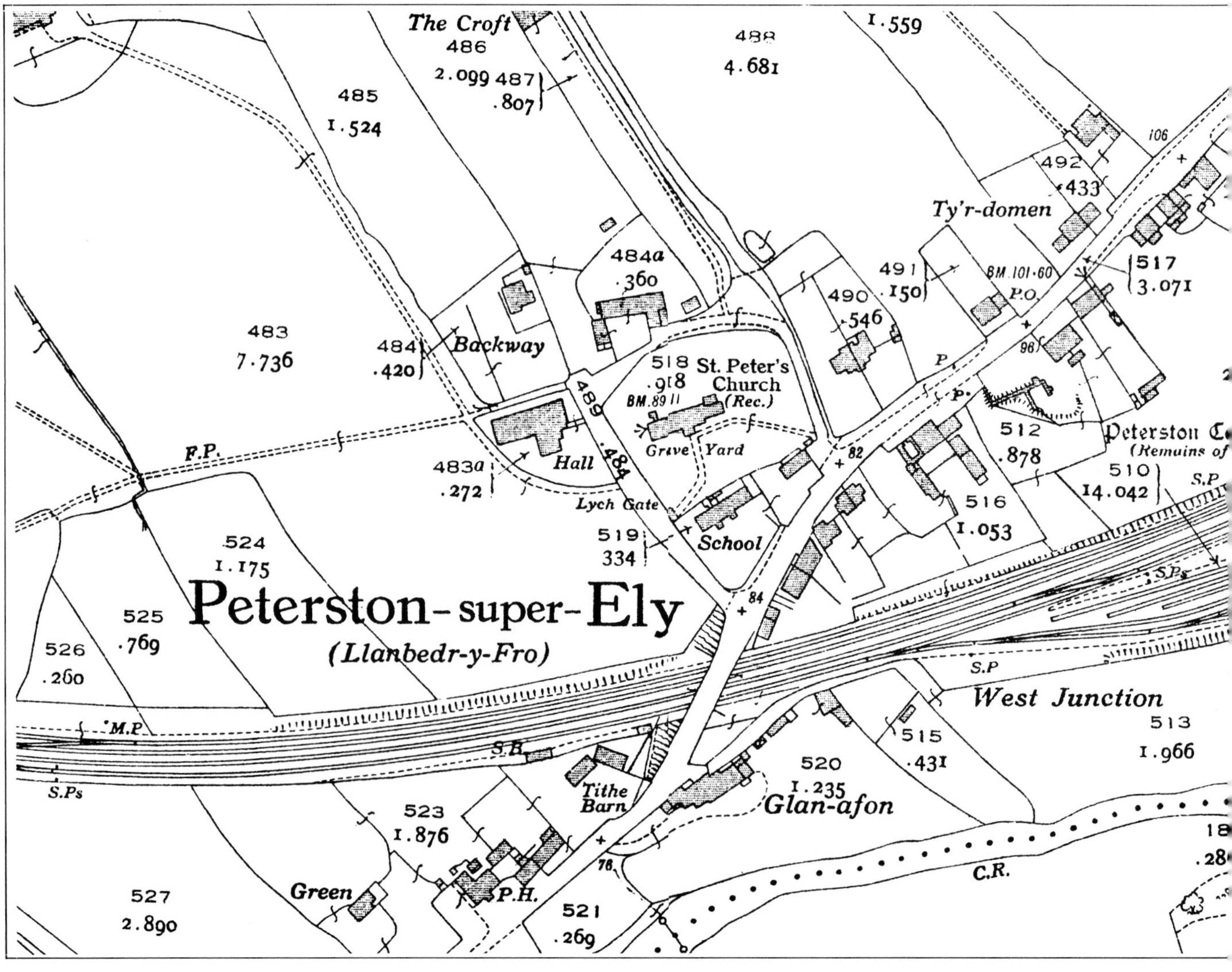

Another sweeping curve brings the line to Peterston, where the Barry Railway again featured significantly. Opening their lines in 1889, the Barry Railway also acquired a double junction at Peterston with the South Wales Main Line for connections to and from the west. On the down side of the Great Western main line, they laid in a total of five sidings, on both sides of their running lines to Drope Junction, while the Great Western provided new signal boxes at Peterston East and West in June 1889 (both actually being to the east of the station, the box names relating to the yard connections). In 1896, up and down loops were provided between the two boxes, and these were extended in 1922 to a point near the eastern end of the passenger station; the existing Peterston West signal box was closed at this time, and a new box opened a little further west along the down loop. Peterston passenger station was officially closed in November 1964, though its name had been removed from public timetables in 1959, and thereafter it was used for one morning pick-up and one evening set-down only. Peterston East box closed in July 1964, when the connections into the east end sidings and goods loops (except part of the up loop) were removed, and the West box (along with the shortened up goods loop) in April 1966, when full MAS operated. Use of the former Barry Railway line and yard diminished with the reduction in shipment coal to Barry Docks, and they were closed in March 1962, though remaining for storage of condemned wagons until July 1964. A few excursions from Llantrisant, Tonyrefail and Penygraig and from the Bridgend Valleys still ran that way to Barry Island until Summer 1961. A goods yard with two sidings (each equipped with a cattle dock) was provided behind the down platform, and though facilities became restricted, it remained in situ until 1964.

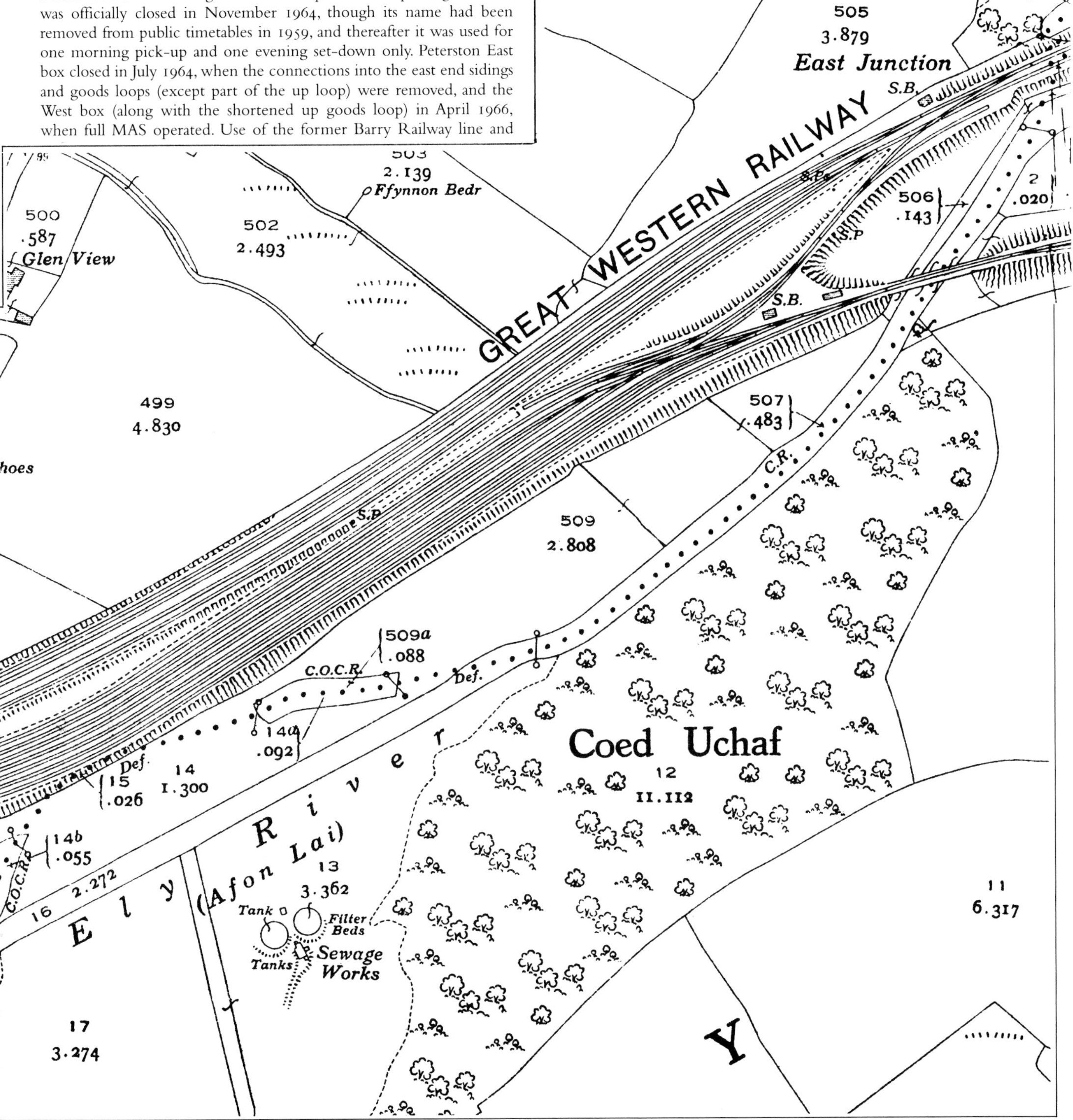

Taken from 25-inch Ordnance Survey for 1942. (Crown copyright reserved)

Peterston East, with diesel railcar No. 3 rounding the bend to the east of the station, probably in 1952. In the early 1950s, there were two fast diesel workings from Cardiff to Swansea, leaving General station at 2.0 and 4.8 p.m.; No. 3 is probably seen here on the former service. The up and down loop lines are clearly seen on either side of the mains, together with the intermediate connection from the down loop to the down main, which enabled a higher-priority freight to overtake a lower-priority one standing in advance on the down loop, a feature that was also available on the up loop. Also shown on the right is the connection from the former Barry Railway sidings into the down loop and down main lines.

G. W. TRUST

The tight curve through Peterston is well illustrated by this shot of Landore 'Castle' No. 5077 *Fairey Battle* as it passed over the road bridge at the east end of the station with the 11.55 a.m. Paddington to Pembroke Dock and Milford Haven during the summer of 1960. There was a 60 mph restriction around the curve for ¾-mile, the section extending westwards from West Junction, through the station, to a point some ¼-mile beyond. The signal on the left of the bracket controlled entrance to the up loop, whilst that to the right of the train controlled the exit from the down loop, both loops comfortably holding two lengthy trains. Each loop was provided with an intermediate connection into the main, enabling one goods train to pass another. Further around the curve, on the right, were the Barry Sidings, which were connected to that former company's Pontypridd & Cadoxton line at Drope Jct.

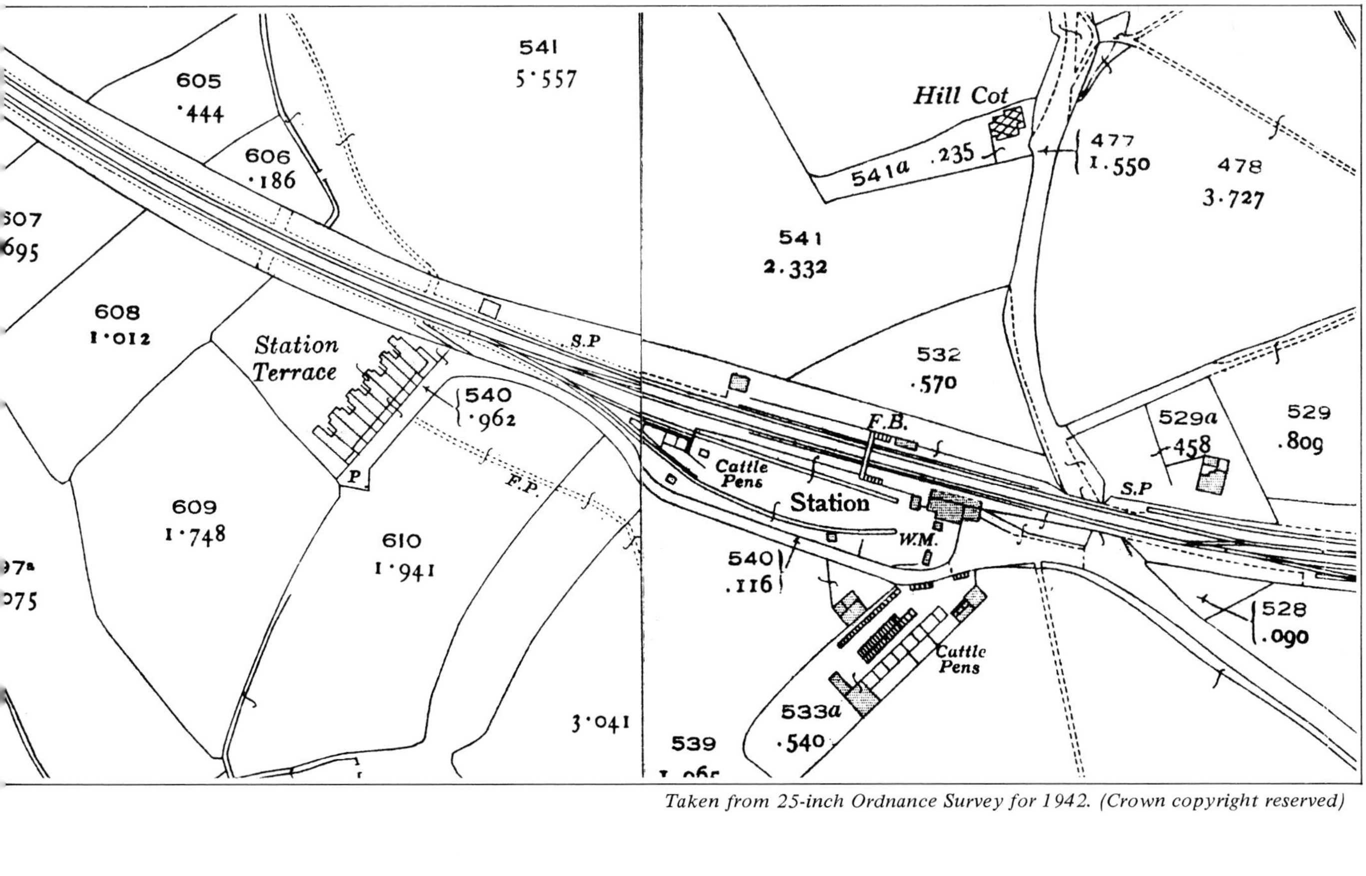

Taken from 25-inch Ordnance Survey for 1942. (Crown copyright reserved)

No. 3440 *City of Truro* and Gloucester 'Mogul' No. 4358 with the return working of the Ian Allan 'Daffodil Express', running eastwards along the main line on 18th May 1957. This special had worked westwards along the Vale of Neath route, and is seen here returning eastwards along the main line. The train is nicely lit by the evening sun, with Pontsarn Crossing box in the distance. R. O. TUCK

PONTSARN TO MISKIN

Canton 'Castle' No. 5095 *Barbury Castle* heading through Pontsarn on 12th May 1958 with the 10.35 a.m. Kensington to Whitland, on that day a light train of eight empty milk tanks and brake van. Ro-rail tanks can be seen near the front of the train. R.O.TUCK

Only a mile-and-a-half further west of Peterston, another pair of loops was situated between Pontsarn and Miskin. At Pontsarn, the line crossed the River Ely, and when the loops were installed in 1914, their eastern end was just to the west of that river bridge. At that time, the controlling box was named Duffryn Bridge, and stood on the down side of the line on the north bank of the river. The loops were then 51 chains long (down) and 54 (up), but in 1921 these were each lengthened over the river bridge by another 34 chains.

Duffryn Bridge box was closed in January 1921 and re-opened further east as Pontsarn Crossing, located near the level crossing, 7 chains beyond the new east end of the loops. With the introduction of MAS in April 1964, both loops were cut back to their original length and the box taken out of use, automatic half barriers being provided for the level crossing, with instructions for the drivers of heavy or slow-moving vehicles to contact Cardiff Panel to obtain permission before crossing.

At the west end of the loops was Miskin Crossing box, which records show was in existence in 1898. The box stood at 179m 58ch and remained in use until the introduction of MAS in April 1964 when it was reduced to a ground frame; this was itself removed when the level crossing was closed in 1978, the road across the line being closed and upgraded with a re-routing to Junction 34 on the new M4 Motorway.

With a heavy load of 17 loaded tanks and van, Swindon 'Castle' No. 5095 *Shrewsbury Castle* is seen here passing Pontsarn with the 3.50 p.m. Whitland to Kensington milk on 12th May 1958. This train might have exceeded the 500-ton mark, which was the maximum for a milk, fish or parcels service with a 'Castle', running between Swansea and Cardiff. Once more, a couple of Ro-rail tankers had been marshalled into the train. The use of powerful passenger engines on the milk services was determined by the importance of the traffic, the required speeds, and the weight of the loaded trains, with each 3,000-gallon tank at around 28 tons and the brake van with churns at even more. The signal box can be seen on the down side in the distance beyond the end of the train. R. O. TUCK

I visited Pontsarn one late-spring evening in 1960 and took a number of views from the signal box at the east end of the loops. This view shows the 2.30 p.m. Neyland to Paddington (5.30 p.m. ex-Swansea, 7.0 p.m. Cardiff) approaching the box on the up main, and passing over the trailing crossover between the main lines, from which it was possible to enter the down goods loop. The engine was the. 1949-built 'Castle' No. 7021 *Haverfordwest Castle* from Landore shed, displaying its trademark silver buffers.

Canton 'Britannia' No. 70029 *Shooting Star* approaching Pontsarn box, passing the down bracket signal with arms for the main line and the loop. The train was the 3.55 p.m. Paddington to Fishguard Harbour, which was due into Fishguard at 10.40 p.m. to connect with the 11.45 p.m. sailing to Cork (Penrose Quay). The sea journey was 140 nautical miles (161 statute miles) and Cork was reached at about 9.0 a.m. the following morning.

The 3.50 p.m. Whitland to Kensington milk that evening was hauled by Old Oak 'Castle' No. 5014 *Goodrich Castle*, reputedly one of the poorer performing London 'Castles'. The train, which comprised 14 tanks and a passenger brake van, had just passed the loops between Miskin and Pontsarn. The bridge under the rear of the train carried the railway over the Ely River, which had kept close company with the railway from the outskirts of Cardiff.

The signalman's view, showing a train of prefabricated bullhead track sections behind a 72XX 2–8–2T, which was turned into the Pontsarn down goods loop a few yards ahead. A 'prefab' PW depot was opened at Radyr to construct track sections. and the train may have originated there.

In addition to expresses to and from London, the Midlands and the North, the section between Cardiff and Swansea also saw fast trains from the West Country and Bristol to either Swansea or Carmarthen, calling only at principal stations. This view shows Canton 'Britannia' No. 70016 *Ariel* heading the 5.0 p.m. Bristol to Swansea on the approach to Pontsarn box in the spring of 1960. The train carried a buffet car from Bristol, and through coaches from Weston-super-Mare.

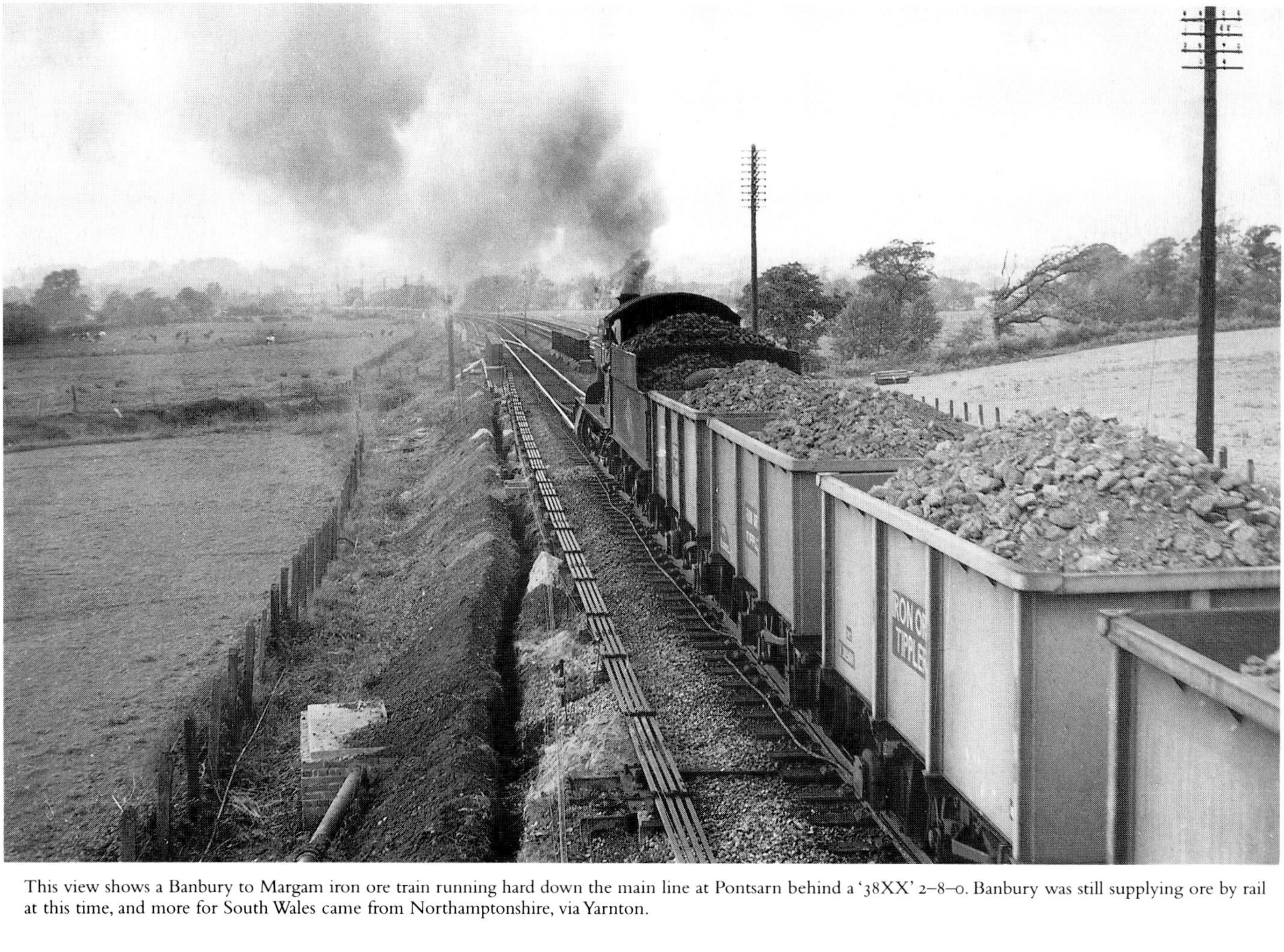

This view shows a Banbury to Margam iron ore train running hard down the main line at Pontsarn behind a '38XX' 2–8–0. Banbury was still supplying ore by rail at this time, and more for South Wales came from Northamptonshire, via Yarnton.

Crossing the Ely River at Miskin, on the approach to Llantrisant, Old Oak Common 'Castle' No. 5034 *Corfe Castle* is seen with a down evening express service on Sunday, 6th May 1956; this train was probably the 4.55 p.m. Paddington to Swansea, a regular Sunday turn for Old Oak shed in the winter schedule of 1955/6. The engine returned to London the following day with the 1.10 p.m. Pembroke Dock (3.50 p.m. Swansea) to Paddington.

LLANTRISANT

Llantrisant Station stood at 181m 37ch and was a major junction with branch lines radiating north westwards to Mwyndy Junction (where they split for Pontypridd and Penygraig, and again subsequently for mineral lines), and south-westwards to Cowbridge and Aberthaw.

After the opening of the South Wales Railway in 1850, the Ely Valley line was the first on the scene, opening between Llantrisant and Tonyrefail in August 1860, and on to Penygraig in December 1862. In January 1862, a branch was opened off this line at Mwyndy Junction, which in the following year was to reach Pontypridd via a new connection into the Taff Vale main line at Treforest, to become the Llantrisant & Taff Vale Junction Railway. Opened initially for goods only, passenger services through to Pontypridd did not commence until January 1875. A multitude of short branch lines serving local collieries sprang up off both the Penygraig and Pontypridd routes, via Gellyrhaidd Jct. and Gilfach Jct. off the Penygraig line, and via Maesaraul Jct., Common Branch Jct. and Treferig Jct. off the Pontypridd line, which, with other lines also feeding in, created a complicated network of essentially mineral lines throughout the Ely Valley.

The east end of Llantrisant station, looking west on Saturday, 5th May 1951, with the island platform building and East box's signals framed by the arch of the bridge. The presence of the Ely Valley line is announced by the inclusion of Tonyrefail and Penygraig on the station nameboard, but the Cowbridge and Pontypridd branches were not included, though both of these would soon close to passengers.
H. C. CASSERLEY

Llantrisant Station, looking east from the end of the up platform in 1963. Though the down platform was an island, the tracks on its south side, running here between the platform and the retaining wall, with the buffer stop in the distance, were only a dead-end siding, intended for use by the original Cowbridge branch trains. They were never connected with the down main.
LENS OF SUTTON

'Grange' No. 6828 *Trellech Grange* from Llanelly shed passing through Llantrisant with the 9.10 a.m. Birmingham to Pembroke Dock, running under clear signals on Saturday, 13th July1957. The 9.10 a.m. Birmingham to Pembroke Dock (12.35 p.m. Cardiff), was rostered for a Landore engine (outbound working, the 9.5 a.m. Swansea to Cardiff). Pannier No. 4674 in the bay platform was preparing to depart with the next Penygraig service, the 1.10 p.m. (SO) from Llantrisant.
S. RICKARD

In February 1865, the Taff Vale Railway opened a branch to Cowbridge, and extended this to Aberthaw in October 1892 to take advantage of the port facilities available there.

A map of the Llantrisant layout in 1876, four years after the abandonment of the broad gauge, shows the station comprising two short platforms, an up platform apparently only for eastward main line services, and a down island platform, the north face for west-bound main line services and the south face for branch services, seemingly used by the Ely Valley and Taff Vale services jointly, with a turntable at the east end. A South Wales Railway goods shed was located on the up side, just west of the up platform.

Llantrisant East Signal Box was located on the down side at the junction of the Ely Valley branch with the main line, and directly behind it was the Taff Vale box controlling the Cowbridge single-line branch. Within the triangle formed by the two diverging branches was a nest of some eight sidings – mostly on the north side of the main line, the most southerly of which was a private siding dating from 1876 for the Ely Tinplate Company, whose factory dominated the down side between the main line and the Cowbridge branch. Another signal box, controlling the Mwyndy line, was located about 15 chains west of the East box along the branch, and was also responsible for movements in and out of the engine shed located in the curve of the Mwyndy branch as it ran north-west. Finally, Llantrisant West Signal Box was located 31 chains to the west of the East box, on the down side of the main line at Tan-y-Bryn level crossing.

In 1891, a new junction for the Ely Valley branch with the main line was laid in, and a new station built with longer platforms, though their use appears to have been the same as previously, with Mwyndy line trains having to cross the junction into and out of the south face of the island platform. By 1894, the TVR had added their own goods facilities, and in 1897 replaced their signal box with a new one. In 1896, a new private siding (in the name of T. J. Masters) to service Llanelay Colliery was opened at the west end of the sidings, north of the main line, while two new private siding connections into Ely Tinplate Works were also opened.

Large-scale alterations were made at Llantrisant in 1901. A new and enlarged goods shed replaced the previous structure, and this was located further to the west making room for the installation of a new up bay platform for the Penygraig and Pontypridd services, to obviate the need for them to cross the main line. A new 3-road engine shed, complete with new turntable, was built to replace the previous one, and was relocated slightly to the north to enable a new nest of 12 branch sidings to be laid in on either side of the curving Mwyndy branch, 7 on the north side and 5 on the south. This now allowed coal traffic to be marshalled at the main-line access point, and enabled through trains to be held clear of the main line without delaying the branch passenger services. An up goods loop was also created between Llantrisant West and East boxes.

Between 1901 and the grouping in 1922, the only significant alteration to the layout was the creation of a down goods loop from the original siding next to the down main line. Llanelay Colliery passed into various hands, being bought by the Ynysarwed Colliery Co. in 1916, the Cardiff Navigation Colliery Co. in 1921, and the Bargoed Coal Co. in 1923, before finally closing in 1936, the trackwork being recovered in 1938. With the grouping, the GWR closed the former TVR goods shed in June 1922 and the signal box in 1923. The

With all signals off, Canton '42XX' 2–8–0T No. 4270 is seen here trundling through Llantrisant station with the 2.40 p.m. Penarth Curve (Cardiff) to Tondu Class 'J' freight, target H17, in July 1950. At Llanharan, the train would cross from the main line onto the Ogmore branch and run into the north end of Tondu yard, put off its train and then return to Cardiff from the south end of the yard via Bridgend station; this routeing enabled tender engines to be used on the duty, which did not require the engine to be turned at Tondu. The engine was one of the '42s' running without outside steam pipes.
G. W. SHARPE COLLECTION

Landore 'Hall' No. 6918 *Sandon Hall* easing into the up platform at Llantrisant on Saturday, 14th December 1957 with the 12.45 p.m. Swansea to Hereford train. This train called at all stations to Cardiff, then Marshfield, Newport, Pontypool Road and all stations to Hereford, making 26 intermediate stops, and was due at 4.45 p.m. The engine would work this service to Cardiff, returning with the 7.55 a.m. Penzance (4.5 p.m. Cardiff), which ran non-stop to Swansea in total contrast to its outbound working. HUGH DAVIES

An unusual job for Canton Pannier No. 9723, which was more likely to be found on station pilot at the General station than working the 12.20 p.m. (SO) Cardiff to Porthcawl stopping passenger service on 13th July 1957, probably indicating that the usual Ebbw Jcn. 2–6–2T had failed or was not otherwise available. The departure from Llantrisant was 12.39 p.m. and the train is seen drawing away from the down platform with all signals off for a clear run ahead to Llanharan. The 12.20 p.m. was sandwiched between the 8.55 a.m. Paddington and the 9.10 a.m. Birmingham, and was just one station ahead of the latter by the time it reached Pyle, for the Porthcawl branch. S. RICKARD

A post-MAS picture of the station, which must have been taken around the time of closure as the platforms were deserted. The station was, however, still intact. The semaphore signals had all been replaced by colour lights, Llantrisant East box being closed in April 1966 with the West box reduced to a ground frame at the same time. Even though the Royal Mint moved to Llantrisant at this time, the Paddington General Manager and Cardiff Divisional Manager maintained that improving freight train speeds between Bridgend and Cardiff took precedence over the future of such intermediate stations, and all were closed between these points.
AUTHOR'S COLLECTION

Llantrisant Pannier No. 5788 taking water at the former Cowbridge branch platform with the empty hopper train for Glamorgan Hematite Quarry, Llanharry. The picture was taken some time between the start of the progressive installation of MAS and the end of steam in the area during October 1964, when the engine shed was closed.
F. K. DAVIES, CTY. G. W. TRUST

An SLS railtour in the early 1950s which included a trip down the Cowbridge branch behind Cathays' '64XX' 0–6–0PT No. 6423, and a pair of ex-Taff Vale trailers (possibly that of July 1952). These vehicles had twin-leaf doors in the centre to the passenger saloons, and were composites, working when new (1907) on the Cowbridge branch. No. 6423 was a long-term Cathays loco, having been transferred there new from Swindon in September 1935, though it did spend short periods at Merthyr; she is seen here off the Cowbridge bay taking water. P. J. GARLAND

The Cowbridge branch train seen on the curve into the Cowbridge bay in July 1950 with '64XX' No. 6409, probably on loan from Newport (Ebbw Jct), and trailer No. W106. Before the First World War, the Taff Vale operated trains through between Pontypridd, Llantrisant and either Cowbridge or Aberthaw. The southern part of the branch between Cowbridge and Aberthaw was closed to passenger traffic in May 1930, and (apart from a short line to the limestone quarry from Cowbridge) to goods in November 1932. During the 1930s, the Great Western ran a couple of Cowbridge autos through to Tonyrefail, though these ceased in the latter part of the decade, and working was confined between Llantrisant and Cowbridge.

Llantrisant Gas Co. took out a private siding on the up side near Llantrisant West in 1929, near to where other small companies had enjoyed private siding facilities since 1894. After indifferent financial returns, the Aberthaw branch was cut back to Cowbridge in 1930.

The post-war years saw the Ely Tinplate Works pass to Richard Thomas & Baldwins in 1946, while the Ely Valley Branch box closed in July 1949. Passenger services on the Cowbridge branch were withdrawn in November 1951, Pontypridd branch services in March 1952, while the Penygraig service succumbed in June 1958, though goods services on all three routes survived into the 1960s. In 1959, the Llantrisant station layout was rationalised by the removal of the up bay and the shortening of the main-line platforms.

The need to improve freight train running between Bridgend and Cardiff saw the closure of two stations east of Llantrisant in September 1962, and though the transfer of the Royal Mint to the town was announced, this did not prevent the closure of Llantrisant itself, together with Peterston and the intermediate stations to the west in 1964. Most collieries in the Ely Valley had closed by this time, leaving only Cwm (accessed via Mwyndy, Maesaraul and Common Branch Junctions) and Coedely (located on the original line to Penygraig); the list of collieries closed during the 1950s and early 60s made a depressing read.

With the introduction of diesel traction in South Wales during the early 1960s, Llantrisant engine shed (with an allocation of pannier tanks and 4200 class 2–8–0Ts) was closed in October 1964, with Class 37s from Canton covering the majority of services still required. Goods traffic was handled direct from Cardiff Goods, though the local goods shed was retained by private contractors. House coal traffic was concentrated at Bridgend and Coity Yard, which became the central point for the area.

The progressive demise of the South Wales coalfield saw Cwm and Coedely collieries and coke ovens closed in 1983, with the branch from Llantrisant taken out in 1984. Traffic from the Llanharry Hematite Quarry on the former Cowbridge branch had lasted until July 1975. Though most of the sidings in the area were progressively recovered, a small yard, accessed through Cardiff Panel, survived. Though not operational on a regular basis, there have been movements in and out from time to time; the logic of retaining this yard may have been to enable the main line to be cleared in case of emergency. On a positive note. with the introduction of the Maesteg to Cardiff DMU service in 1992, a new station was opened at Pontyclun, the main centre of population in the area.

Llantrisant '14XX' No. 1471 standing in the up bay with an Ely Valley train during the mid-1950s. The Penygraig passenger service was withdrawn in June 1958, and No. 1471 was transferred to join a rapidly-diminishing number of her class on auto duties at Exeter. The village of Pontyclun can be seen to the left, though the station was named after Llantrisant, some 1½ miles distant beyond yet another village, Talbot Green.
DAVID LAWRENCE, CTY. HUGH DAVIES

An evening Llantrisant to Pontypridd auto train standing in the up bay, formed with a two-coach low-roof ex-TV trailer set (with No. W1317 at the rear), and a '56XX' engine at the head. The 9¼-mile journey to Pontypridd via Cross Inn and Tonteg took around a half-hour. IAN L. WRIGHT

A view looking west from Llantrisant up platform in July 1950. The ex-Aberthaw branch may be seen on the extreme left, curving around on its southerly course for Cowbridge, by that time the end of the line. Llantrisant East box is seen to the left, and in the distance on the right, the goods shed. A little beyond that shed, curving to the right, was the branch serving the Ely Valley (Penygraig) and Pontypridd lines, which parted company around the bend at Mwyndy Jct. With the platform lamp, two underslung backing signals, water crane and bay signals ('bay' clearly marked on the starter), the end of the platform was full of interest.
P. J. GARLAND

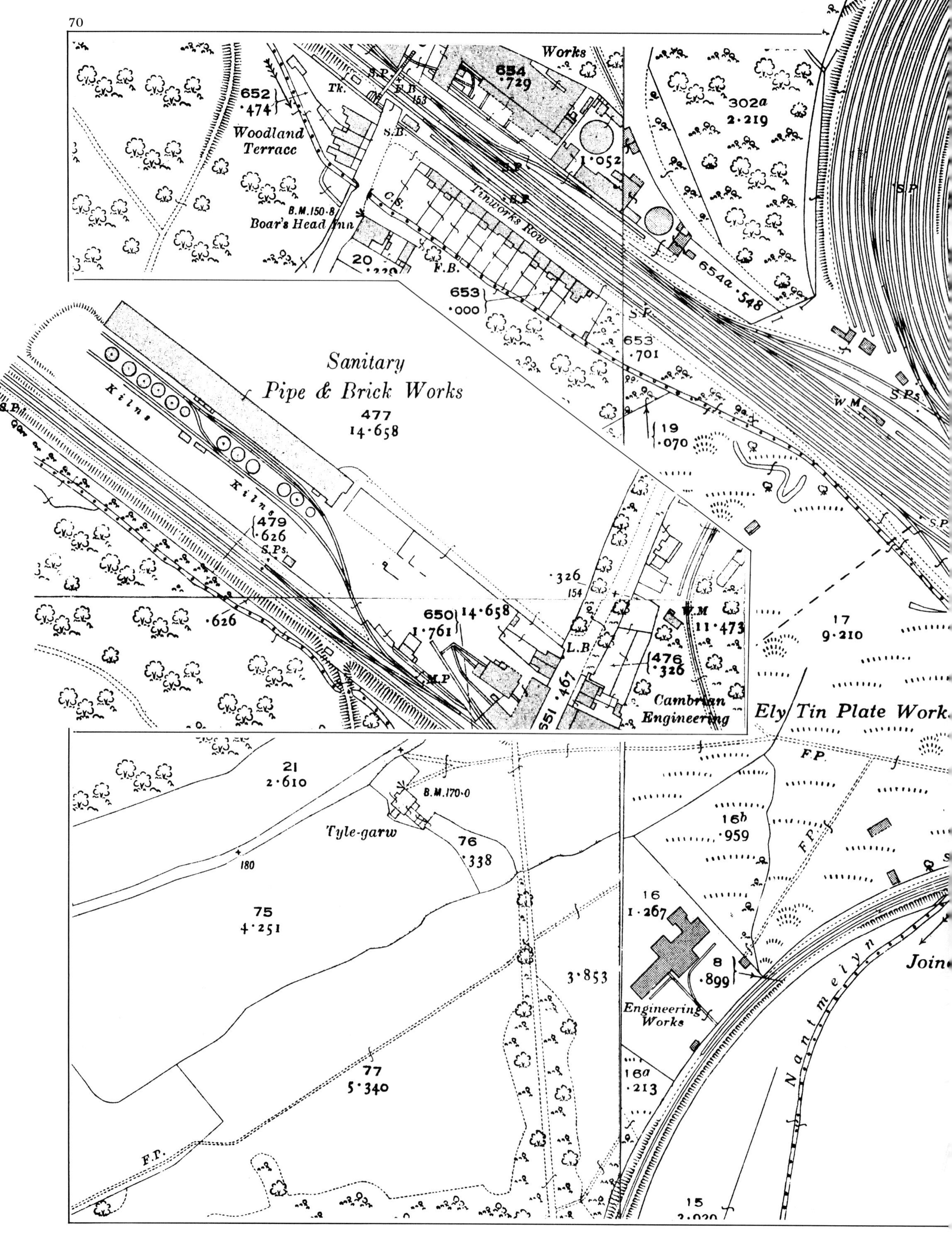

Works
654
·729
652
·474
Tk.
S.P.
F.B.
153
Woodland
Terrace
S.B.
302a
2·219
1·052
B.M.150·8
Boar's Head Inn
C.S.
Tinworks Row
20
F.B.
653
·000
654a ·548
653
·701
Sanitary
Pipe & Brick Works
477
14·658
Kilns
Kilns
S.P.
W.M
S.Ps.
19
·070
479
·626
S.Ps.
·326
154
·626
650
1·761
14·658
L.B.
W.M
11·473
17
9·210
476
·326
551 ·467
M.P
Cambrian
Engineering
Ely Tin Plate Work
21
2·610
B.M.170·0
F.P.
Tyle-garw
76
·338
180
16b
·959
F.P.
75
4·251
16
1·267
8
·899
3·853
Engineering
Works
Nantmelyn
77
5·340
16a
·213
F.P.
15

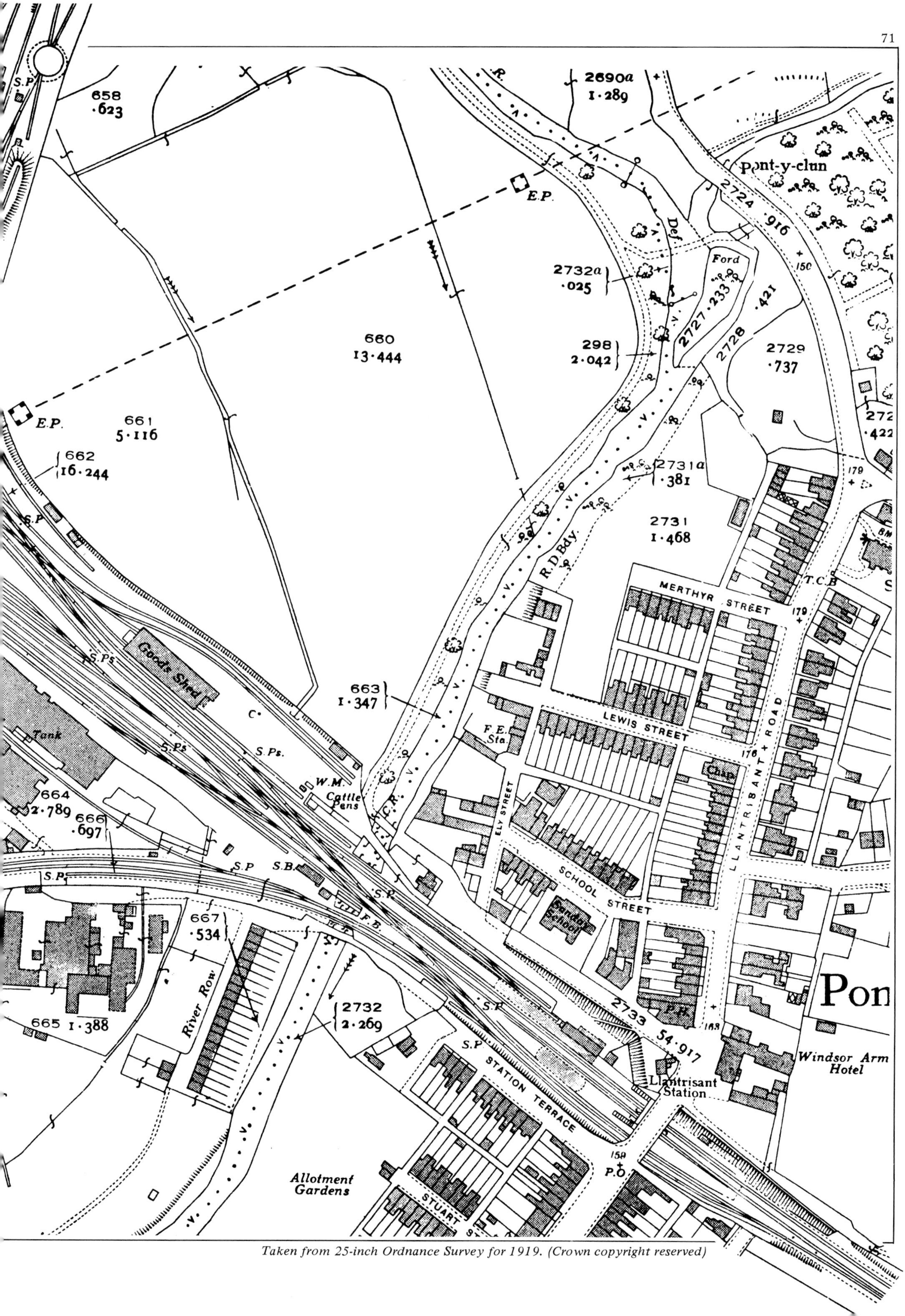

Taken from 25-inch Ordnance Survey for 1919. (Crown copyright reserved)

The single auto coach W255W for Penygraig leaving Llantrisant bay platform, but not with an auto-equipped engine, which was probably under repair. The engine on this Saturday, 13th July 1957, was Pannier No. 4674, based at Llantrisant, but more used to shunting and trip working than branch passenger. The auto coach was one of a batch of former brake third, hauled-stock, converted to auto coaches in 1955, and differed from the traditional trailers in having five compartments instead of saloons, with a significant van area.

S. RICKARD

Llantrisant shed was a 'northlight' pattern three-road structure, located on the inside of the curve between the station and Mwyndy Jct. box, along with a 55ft turntable, coal stage and the usual facilities. It housed the power required for branch passenger, freight and shunting operations, although its engines were also used for duties to Cardiff and, when required, to Margam. In this view, the shed is seen on Saturday, 5th May 1951, along with a typical selection of motive power. By this time, No. 1471 had been joined by 1421, one of which can be seen here on the left. in addition to the auto engines, the allocation at Llantrisant included three '42XX' 2–8–0Ts and six '57XX' 0–6–0PTs; two '57s' are seen at the near end of the shed, and a '42' at the far end.
H. C. CASSERLEY

Ex-Alexandra Dock 2–6–2T No. 1205 is seen on shed on 5th June 1948, a year after her transfer down from Newport (Pill), though she moved on to Canton in the winter of 1950/1 to act as shed pilot; No. 1205 was withdrawn from service in January 1956. IAN L. WRIGHT

Llantrisant West on a sunny summer evening, Monday, 1st July 1957 with Swindon 'Castle' No. 5062 *Earl of Shaftesbury* passing with the 3.50 p.m. Whitland to Kensington milk. This engine would soon be re-allocated to Bristol Bath Road, and then, in September 1960 to Landore, where she became a very prized possession, working regularly on the top-link London services, turned out as only Landore knew how. The freight train held on the up loop was awaiting the passage of the milk.

Shortly after the passage of the Whitland milk, the ground vibrated as the 3.45 p.m. Paddington to Fishguard Harbour stormed through behind Canton 'Britannia' No. 70023 *Venus*. The up freight was still held on the up loop.

Another main-line movement in a busy thirty minutes at Llantrisant around 7.0 p.m. was the 3.55 p.m. Paddington to Fishguard Harbour ('Capitals United Express'), seen here behind Canton 'Castle' No. 5030 *Shirburn Castle*. The two Fishguard expresses were scheduled to be 12 minutes apart at this point, but as the 3.55 was due to call at more stations than the 3.45, this time became 37 minutes by the time it reached Fishguard. '42XX' 2–8–0T No. 4236 from Tondu shed was waiting for the road in the down goods loop with a 'K' class freight, possibly a return Cardiff to Tondu working.

A well-turned-out Llanelly 'Hall' No. 4941 *Llangedwyn Hall* speeding on the up main through the western outskirts of Llantrisant with the class 'C' Llandilo Junction to West Midlands train, conveying tinplate from Trostre and Velindre Works for use in the building of yet more cars. It is believed that the vans had reinforced floors to take the traffic, and those formed in the front half of the train appear to be very similar in design.

LLANHARAN

Llanharan is located at the top of the climb from Ely in the east, and Tremains in the west. The existence of sidings serving Meiros (Mayrose) Colliery on the up side, shown on an 1875 map of the area, required a signal box to control access to the main line. The colliery was located a mile or so to the north of the village, and the sidings were situated on the north side of the line, to the east of the Bridgend & Pontypridd road bridge.

In October 1876, a single-line branch to Tondu was opened, with double-line track at the junction, and Llanharan Junction signal box was opened to control access; its name was soon changed to West box, the other box (serving the colliery sidings) then becoming Llanharan East. The East box was renewed in 1897 and sited on the down side, also controlling a newly-provided down refuge siding.

Unlike other stations on the section between Cardiff and Bridgend. Llanharan passenger station and goods facilities were not opened until September 1899, although it is possible that a short-lived colliers platform was provided on the branch just before that.

By 1915 the sidings at Meiros Colliery had been extended, and 1921 saw important alterations with the provision of up and down loops, and a new Llanharan West signal box. Meiros Colliery closed in 1933, and the sidings serving it were recovered.

Llanharan continued untouched for almost 30 years after this until the closure of the passenger station and the Tondu branch in 1964, with goods traffic then delivered from Cardiff. Both signal boxes and running loops were taken out of use when MAS was introduced into the area in 1965, leaving only up and down main lines.

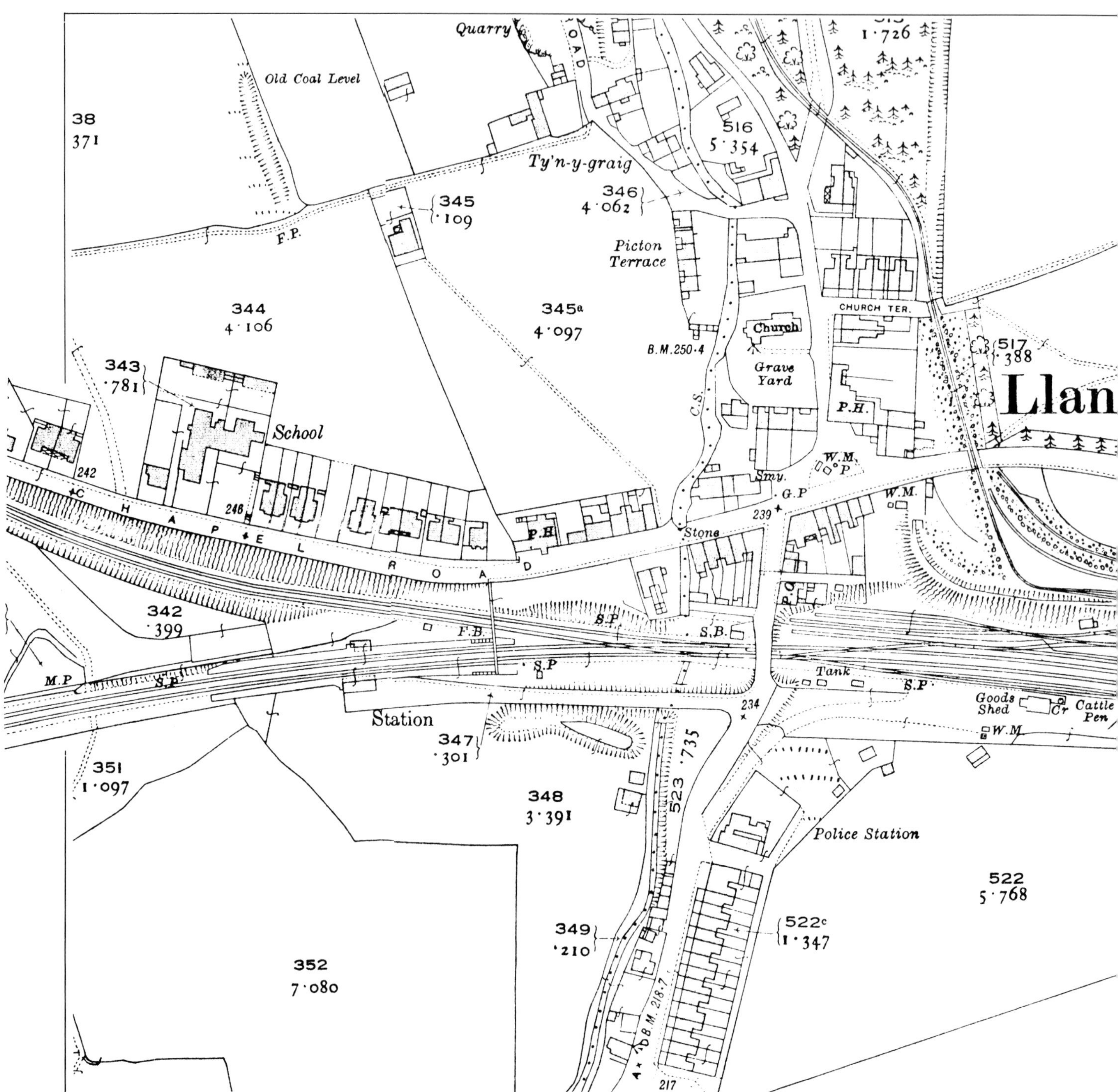

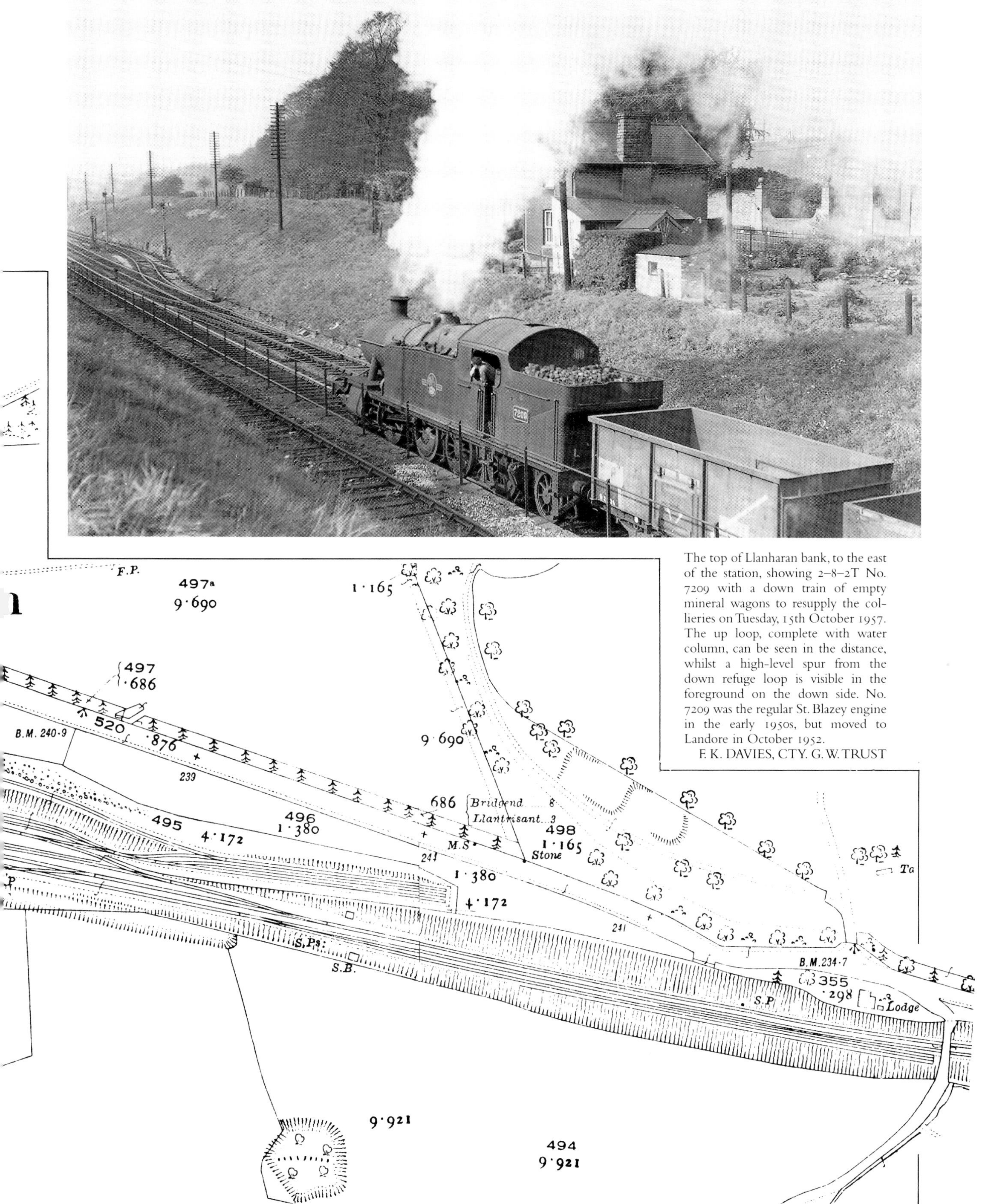

The top of Llanharan bank, to the east of the station, showing 2–8–2T No. 7209 with a down train of empty mineral wagons to resupply the collieries on Tuesday, 15th October 1957. The up loop, complete with water column, can be seen in the distance, whilst a high-level spur from the down refuge loop is visible in the foreground on the down side. No. 7209 was the regular St. Blazey engine in the early 1950s, but moved to Landore in October 1952.

F. K. DAVIES, CTY. G. W. TRUST

Taken from 25-inch Ordnance Survey for 1919. (Crown copyright reserved)

About half-a-mile to the west of the station on the main line was Llanharan Colliery, where the Powell Duffryn Steam Coal Co. opened a private siding in 1921, access from the running lines being controlled by a ground frame. In 1924, the ground frame was replaced by Llanharan Colliery signal box. The NCB ceased production in later years, but the signal box and connections were maintained against future plans to use the site, all however being removed under the introduction of MAS in 1964. However, the NCB did re-open the site as Llanharan Opencast in 1970, and operated it until the end of 1982. The proximity of the underground workings caused regular subsidence problems, and permanent speed restrictions of 40 mph were necessary on the main line for a mile to the west of Llanharan.

Approaching Llanharan Jct on the down main, c.1952, with the goods loops to the left and right of the running lines, and the small goods yard on the extreme left. The former connections with the Meiros Colliery (closed 1933) were off the up goods loop, to the right. Beyond the road bridge, the double track of the Ogmore branch can be seen diverging off to the right, whilst the main line continued its curve to the left through the station. New support pillars had been constructed under the bridge. P. J. GARLAND

Llanharan West signal box, situated tight against the roadbridge, on 28th July 1963. In addition to controlling access to and from the Tondu branch, the box also controlled entry to and exit from the west ends of the up and down goods loop lines, which ran for some 30 chains to the east of the bridge. The east end of these loops was controlled by Llanharan East box, which, because it was also required to control the connections into Meiros Colliery, was located some 11 chains west of the far end of the loops. Both boxes closed on 27th June 1965 with the introduction of MAS into the area. COLLECTION ROGER CARPENTER

Llanharan station on 28th July 1963, looking towards Bridgend with, on the right, the remains of the Llanharan to Tondu branch which was closed on 3rd December 1962. The double junction that formed the connections with the main lines had been removed. The branch was double track beyond the junction, but became single after 23 chains (some 500 yards). Access from the main part of the village could be gained by means of the footbridge, which crossed all four running lines and served both platforms. The small arm on the bracket signal in the right foreground controlled entry into the up loop.
COLLECTION ROGER CARPENTER

The east end of Llanharan station on 28th July 1963, showing Llanharan West signal box, which previously controlled access to and from the Tondu branch behind the station. Its sighting to the east under the road bridge had not been improved by the provision of additional support pillars under the bridge. The barrow load of milk churns awaiting the arrival of the next down stopping passenger service is indicative of the era.
COLLECTION ROGER CARPENTER

Llanharan station, looking west from the down platform towards Pencoed on 28th July 1963, by which time only the intermediate stations at Pencoed, Llanharan and Llantrisant remained open for traffic. Access was by road on the down side of the station, off the A473 Pontypridd to Bridgend road that crossed over the line just to the east of the station. The main line station did not open until 1899, although it is believed that a colliery platform may have briefly existed on the branch alongside before that time. Llanharan station was closed for traffic in November 1964.
COLLECTION ROGER CARPENTER

BRYN-Y-GWYNON

There was originally a siding on the up side at Bryn-y-Gwynon serving the Brynna Colliery, re-opened in 1915 and closed in 1936. Colliers' platforms. were located on the up and down sides of the line, coming into use in 1918, but there is no record available of when these facilities were removed after closure in 1936. The signal box was reduced to a ground frame controlling the level crossing in June 1965 with the introduction of MAS, and the line is now surrounded by woodland, though with a main road nearby.

The main line through the shallow Ewenny Valley skirts some lovely wooded areas. In this view, Canton 'Castle' No. 5030 *Shirburn Castle* is captured speeding west through Bryn-y-Gwynon with the 3.45 p.m. Paddington to Fishguard Harbour, a limited-stop service for travellers to Ireland, on Wednesday, 21st August 1957. The train stopped to pick up (only) at Newport and Cardiff, then called at Swansea and Clarbeston Road en route. At this time, the boat from Fishguard served Waterford on Monday, Wednesday and Friday nights, and Cork on Tuesdays, Thursdays and Saturdays. The Waterford journey was 92 nautical (106 statute) miles, considerably less than to Cork.

Swindon's 'Castle' No. 5025 *Chirk Castle* working hard past Bryn-y-Gwynon with the heavy 3.50 p.m. Whitland to Kensington (and Wood Lane) milk service on 21st August 1957. The depot at Wood Lane was completed in 1935 by United Dairies, spreading over 7½ acres of ground near the White City stadium, and at the time was claimed to be the largest and most up-to-date milk depot in the world. The establishment at Whitland was a milk 'concentration depot', similar to others at Maiden Newton, Yetminster and Wootton Bassett operating in the 'thirties. In 1957, the train firstly called at Wood Lane soon after midnight, then continued the short distance on to Kensington (Olympia). The long shadows of the photographer and his father, cast by the evening sun, are apparent here.

PENCOED

The line curved gently through Pencoed, where all signals were off for the 3.55 p.m. Paddington to Fishguard Harbour ('Capitals United Express') behind Landore Castle' No. 7003 *Elmley Castle*, as it approached the station on Wednesday, 21st August 1957. In common with other named expresses, the train was formed with chocolate and cream stock, in this instance all Mark 1. Because of the curve, the down main signal was located on the up side to afford a better view for drivers (unless, of course, an up train was passing), with East box's distant below.

A map for 1883 shows up and down passenger platforms, with a siding on the up side owned by the Pencoed Brick and Tile Co. The level crossing at the east end of the platforms survives to this day, and the signal box there was renewed and moved to the east edge of the up platform around 1905. A map for 1906 shows an extensive layout of sidings completed in 1901 on land on the up side behind the platform, giving access to a foundry originally owned by Howells, then purchased by the GWR in 1926 before being taken over by Davis Bros. until the foundry closed in 1935, when the layout was removed. An up running loop was brought into use in October 1914, and a down loop in March 1923. The up loop was shortened at the west end in 1961 and both loops were taken out of use, together with the station sidings, under the introduction of MAS in 1965, after which only the running lines remained. The passenger station was closed in November 1964 but re-opened in 1992 with the introduction of the Cardiff & Maesteg service.

A view of Pencoed station, looking east towards Llanharan on 28th July 1963, showing the level crossing and East signal box at the far end of the platform. Pencoed opened rather earlier than its neighbour, Llanharan, in September 1850, just after the line itself was opened for traffic. The 186¾ (186/111) milepost, seen under the up platform nameboard, marked the distance via Gloucester; that via the 'Bristol loop' (Bath and Stapleton Road) was fifteen miles shorter than this, and via Badminton, 25 miles less.
COLLECTION
ROGER CARPENTER

A close-up view of the west end of the station, showing main station building, level crossing and signal box, with the up main starter underslung beneath a bracket to clear the bottom of the footbridge. The building on the down platform immediately to the right of the level crossing had a plate attached to the left-hand leaf of the double doors, and doubtless had a specific use.
COLLECTION
ROGER CARPENTER

Pencoed East signal box on 28th July 1963, located at the east end of the up platform, controlling the level crossing and the west end of the up and down loops to the west of the station. Pencoed West box was located just over ¾-mile (67ch) from East box, and controlled the western end of the loops. The road was a minor route from the northern outskirts of Bridgend, via Coity.
COLLECTION
ROGER CARPENTER

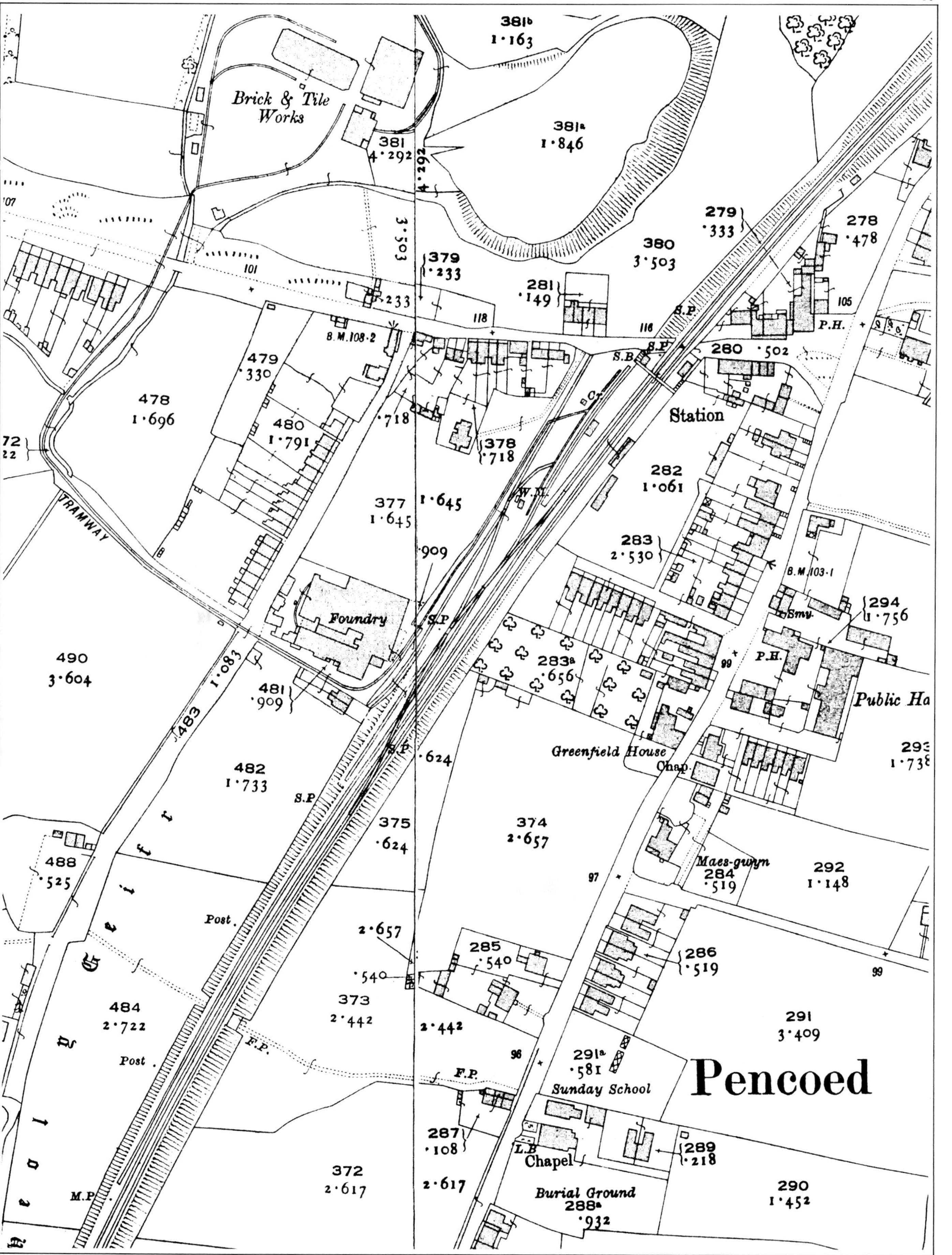

Taken from 25-inch Ordnance Survey for 1936. (Crown copyright reserved)

The view looking west along Pencoed station platforms from the down side. The up yard sidings, behind and beyond the up platform, had a considerable history; they were originally sold to the Pencoed Brick & Tile Co. in a private siding agreement starting in November 1875, and in 1883 the installation passed to Wm. Howells, until 1926, when the land was repurchased by the GWR. The sidings were then let to Davis Bros. from 1928 until their foundry closed in 1935, the chimney in the photograph probably being one of the final vestiges of that era. The up yard sidings survived until the introduction of MAS in 1965. The two home signals in the distance controlled the up main and up goods loop. COLLECTION ROGER CARPENTER

TREMAINS

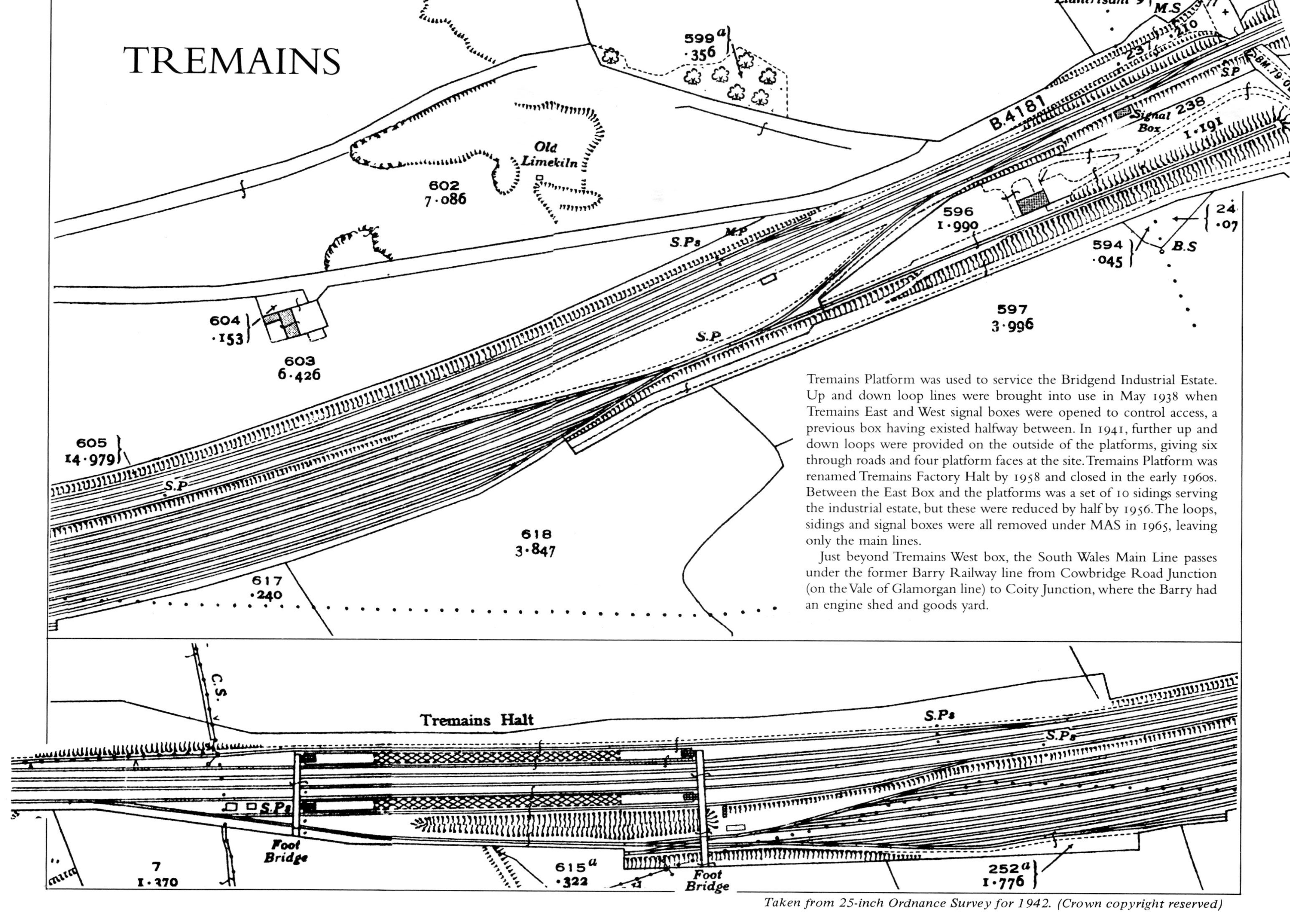

Tremains Platform was used to service the Bridgend Industrial Estate. Up and down loop lines were brought into use in May 1938 when Tremains East and West signal boxes were opened to control access, a previous box having existed halfway between. In 1941, further up and down loops were provided on the outside of the platforms, giving six through roads and four platform faces at the site. Tremains Platform was renamed Tremains Factory Halt by 1958 and closed in the early 1960s. Between the East Box and the platforms was a set of 10 sidings serving the industrial estate, but these were reduced by half by 1956. The loops, sidings and signal boxes were all removed under MAS in 1965, leaving only the main lines.

Just beyond Tremains West box, the South Wales Main Line passes under the former Barry Railway line from Cowbridge Road Junction (on the Vale of Glamorgan line) to Coity Junction, where the Barry had an engine shed and goods yard.

Taken from 25-inch Ordnance Survey for 1942. (Crown copyright reserved)

Landore 'Hall' No. 6903 *Belmont Hall* approaching Bridgend with the 1.0 pm. Cardiff to Swansea stopper on a very bright 23rd November 1957. This train was scheduled for a four-coach corridor set, with three additional Seconds at the rear. The photograph was taken from the B4181 road that crossed over the Vale of Glamorgan and main lines, then under the ex-Barry Railway loop line (to Coity Goods) in the space of a couple of hundred yards.

BRIDGEND

Landore 2–8–2T No. 7209 approaching Bridgend East Jct. with a down class 'H' mixed freight, probably for Swansea or Llandilo Junction, on the afternoon of Saturday, 23rd November 1957. The train is seen passing under the former Barry Railway line from Cowbridge Road Jct. (on the Vale of Glamorgan) to Coity Junction, where the Barry Railway had an engine shed and goods depot (Bridgend & Coity).

The eastern approaches to Bridgend commence at a junction with the original Vale of Glamorgan Railway (worked by the Barry Railway), opened on 1st December 1897, requiring the GWR to open a signal box at Bridgend East. An 1881 map of the railway through Bridgend shows an original Bridgend No. 1 box located towards the east end of the down platform (renamed Bridgend East in 1886), and closed when the new box opened in 1897. Bridgend No. 2 box, renamed Central in 1886 and closed in 1899, was located on the down side beyond the access lines to the goods shed, and also controlled connections between the Tondu line and the main lines. Bridgend No. 3, renamed Llynfi & Ogmore Junction in 1886, controlled access to the engine shed alongside the Tondu branch, the end of the up main line loop and other connections between the main and subsidiary lines, while Bridgend No. 4 box, renamed West in 1886, was on the down side, controlling access to the up loop and crossovers between the main lines. The up platform was an island, used by the Llynfi and Ogmore services on the north side and main line up trains on the south side. The down platform had a bay at the east end, used by the new Vale of Glamorgan services. The engine shed is known to have provided power for the originating Vale of Glamorgan services during the 1920s and 30s and presumably did so when the VoG services started. The same may well have been true for the L&O services.

There were three private sidings at the east end: G. Jenkins & Sons dating from 1862, on the down side, with C. Jenkins and another on the up side, and South Wales Portland Cement just off the end of the up platform. There were two short down loop sidings at the west end of the goods shed, and two short up loops between the West box and the L&O box. The small goods shed on the down side, just beyond the end of the down platform, was extended, as was its servicing siding, in 1899.

By 1890 the up platform had been extended at the west end, whilst the branch platform on the opposite side of the island was extended further, alongside a siding which, trailing from the up line, was used for attaching or detaching tail traffic of up trains.

A map for 1910 shows a connection off the G. Jenkins private siding on the down side at Bridgend East leading to the Bridgend UDC Electricity Works, a wagon works, timber yard and quarry. A further group of private sidings had been created off the down bay loop line, while those on the up side show that the C. Jenkins siding led to a lime kiln, and that of the South Wales Portland Cement to a quarry. The signal boxes had by now been reduced to three: East, Middle (located just west of the up platform) and West, removed from its former position and now located between the main lines and the branch, a new box having opened in 1899. Four new down sidings had been provided, replacing the previous two loop sidings beyond the goods depot. A new private siding named Quarella Siding had opened on the up side, about 15 chains west of the West box, occupied by various undertakings over the years, while further private sidings existed off the L&O line sidings.

By 1955, the private sidings at the east end down side had been taken over by R. S. Hayes Wagon Repairs, while on the up side the Portland Cement siding had gone, and the C. Jenkins siding went in 1954. The single-road engine shed closed in April 1950.

The Blaengarw service ceased in 1953, and that to Nantymoel (the Ogmore branch) in 1958. Bridgend to Abergwynfi trains (Llynvi branch) were diverted from Cymmer to Blaengwynfi and Treherbert upon the closure of Abergwynfi in 1960, and continued thus until withdrawal of the service entirely in 1970; in 1992, the service was partly regenerated by the introduction of a Maesteg to Cardiff service.

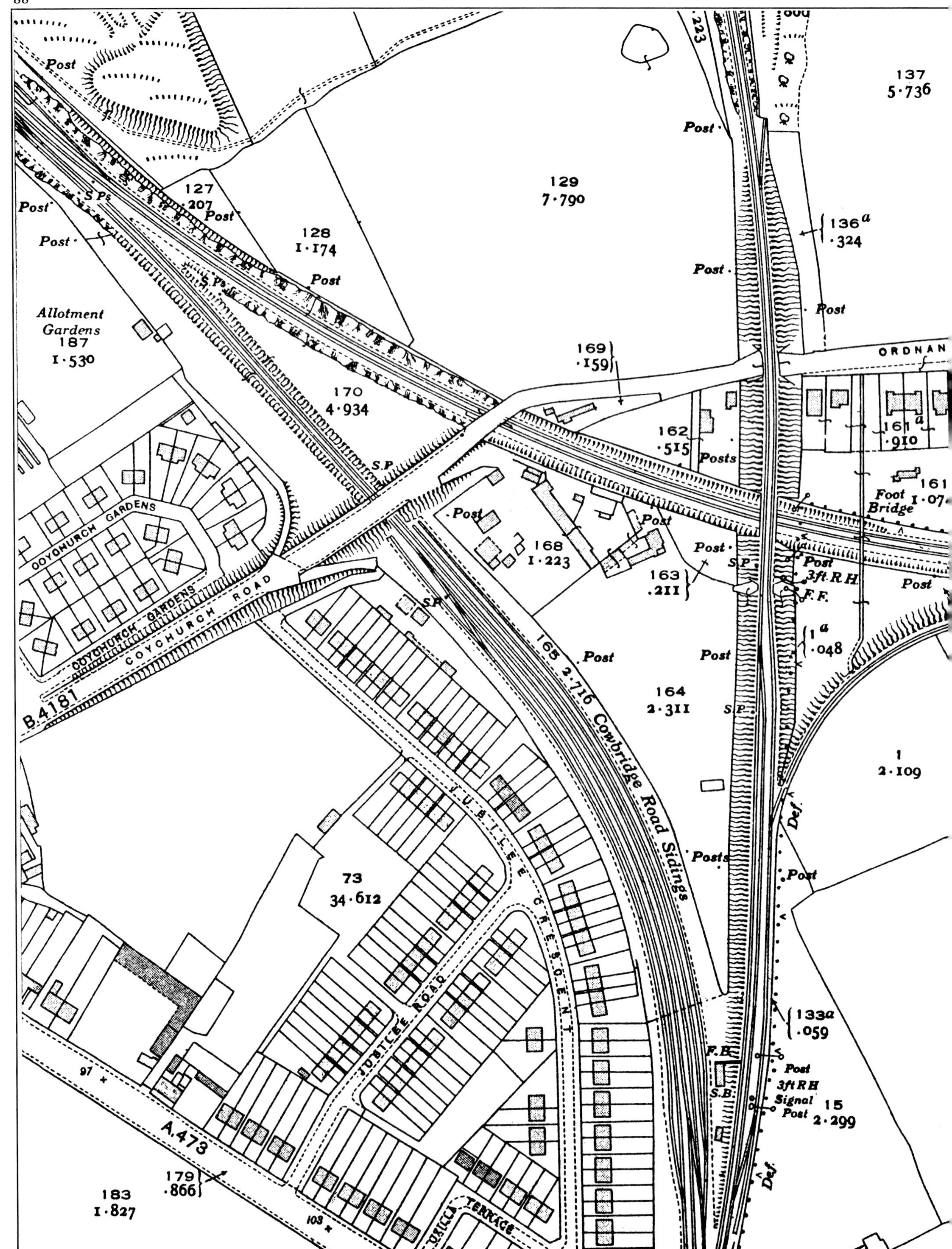

Taken from 25-inch Ordnance Survey for 1940. (Crown copyright reserved)

Vale of Glamorgan passenger services ceased in 1964, but the bay platform line was retained.

MAS was introduced at Bridgend in September 1965, and the three boxes were closed. All connections to the goods shed were severed, the traffic being trunked by road to and from Cardiff Goods. The four down sidings beyond the goods depot were also recovered, as were some loop sidings off the L&O line. The down goods loop also went, but the up loop was retained. The platforms were extended to 840ft by October 1967.

R.S. Hayes became a large-scale scrap dealer for steam engines during the mid 1960s, selling all for scrap and none for preservation, their siding at the east end of the station being closed in September 1969.

By 1979 all the sidings in the station area had been recovered, except two alongside the up goods. The L&O branch was singled, probably from 1983.

The Vale of Glamorgan line remains in use for 'merry-go-round' trains to Aberthaw Power Station, whilst other freight and Post Office Services also use the line daily. It also continues to be used as a diversionary route between Cardiff and Bridgend so that complete blockades for engineering work can take place on the main line. There are plans to re-introduce the passenger train service between Cardiff and Llantwit Major, and this may well involve the service running on to Bridgend, there being a likelihood that the trains will be linked in with other local services to form an attractive through service to and from Cardiff (and possibly Swansea) via the Vale.

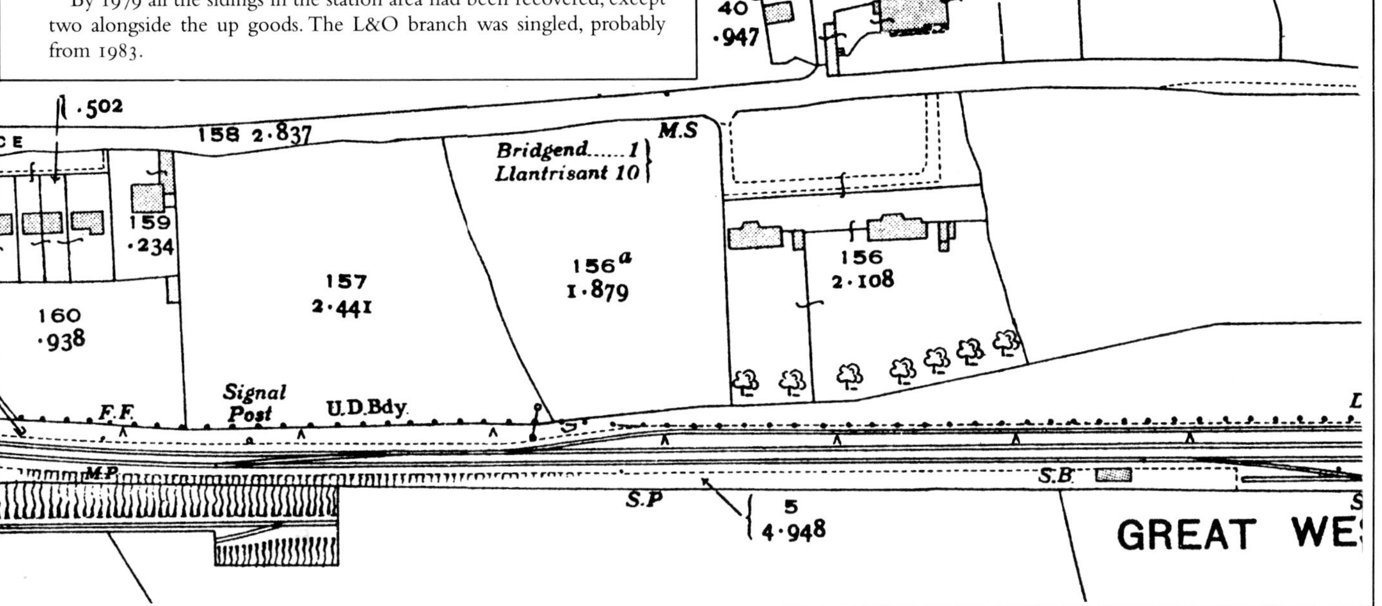

Just slightly further to the east of the location of the previous two pictures, Neyland 'County' No. 1020 *County of Monmouth* is seen at the head of the 8.48 a.m. Fishguard Harbour to Paddington empty vans and parcels service (non-stop through Bridgend) on 23rd November 1957. This train conveyed the returning empty news vans off the 12.45 a.m. Paddington to Carmarthen, and was generally up to full-length limit after Cardiff, such was the demand for accommodation on the service which ran via Gloucester, where stock from overhaul at Gloucester Carriage & Wagon was hard pressed to find room. By the time the train passed Bridgend, the Carmarthen news vans formed the greater part of the train, with a few other vehicles from Fishguard, Carmarthen, Swansea and Neath attached. In the latter 1950s, it carried a non-corridor Van Second coach daily between Fishguard and Gloucester, perhaps for staff use.

Tondu's 0–6–2T No. 6676, getting away in fine style eastwards along the main line from Bridgend around noon on Saturday, 23rd November 1957 with football excursion No. 5 bound for Ninian Park, Cardiff. The six-coach train was formed of Valleys stock. Winter Saturdays saw many football or rugby specials operating within South Wales.

2–8–0T No. 4276 blasting away with an up mineral train, just past the East Junction, where the Vale of Glamorgan line diverged from the main at Bridgend East box, on 23rd November 1957. The leading vehicles at least (other than the two opens on the front) were loaded with coke in the traditional built-up wagons. Around this time, No. 4276 was transferred to Aberbeeg, and would become more at home on the Newport Valleys' trains than main-line work.

Tondu-based '4575' class 2–6–2 auto tank No. 5545, taking water at the east end of Bridgend's Valley platform prior to working the 8.10 p.m. service to Abergwynfi on Monday, 13th July 1959. Bridgend East box can be seen on the right, beyond the road bridge. H. C. CASSERLEY

Canton 'Hall' No. 6932 *Burwarton Hall* waiting at the up platform with a train for Cheltenham on 6th May 1960. The line from the Valleys platform can be seen joining the up main just ahead of the engine. Vale of Glamorgan trains left from the bay on the down side. F. K. DAVIES, CTY. G. W. TRUST

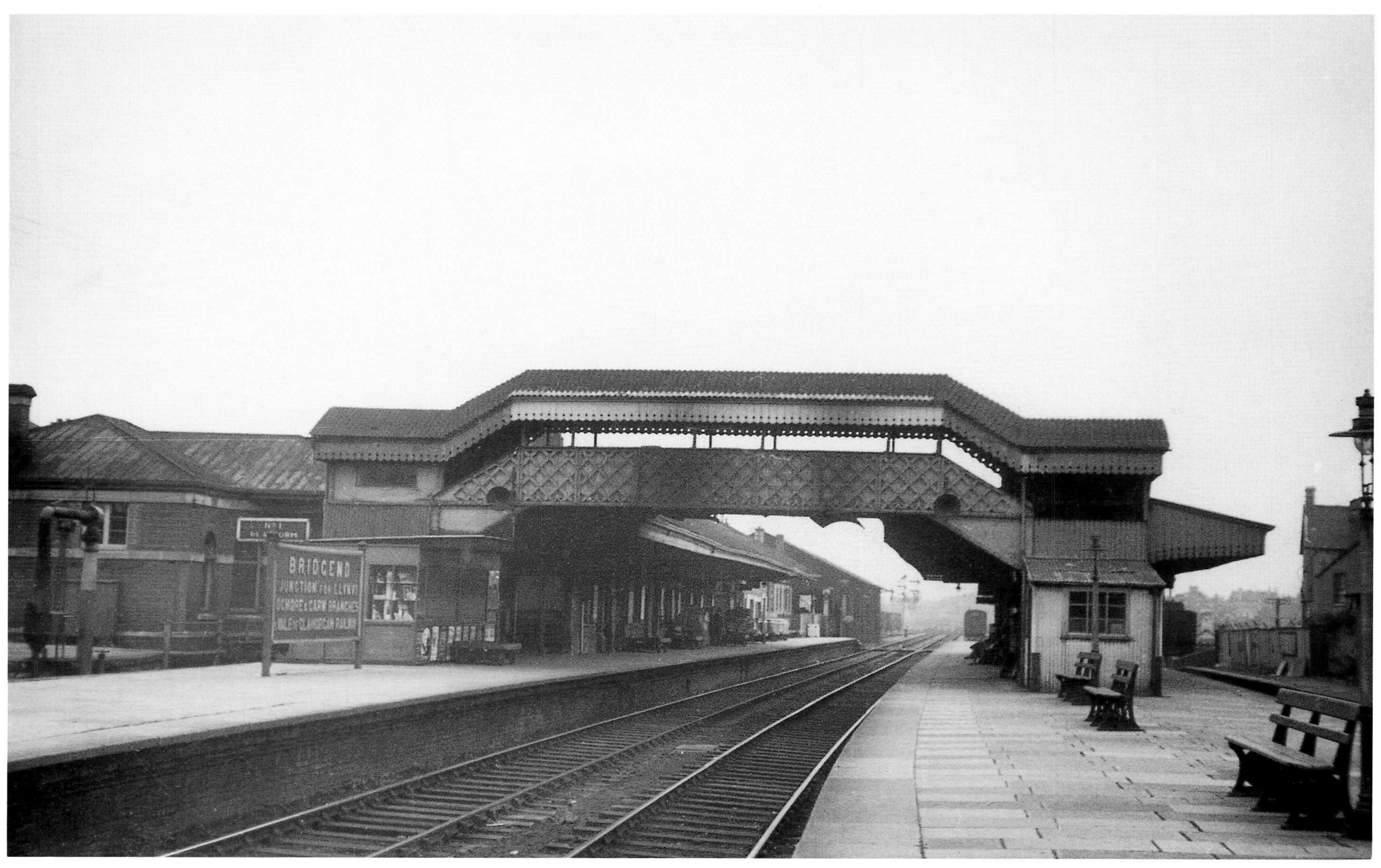

A view along the main platforms looking west on 9th September 1951, showing the large station nameboard at the east end of the down platform. This showed Bridgend as the 'Junction for the Llynfi, Ogmore and Garw Branches and Vale of Glamorgan Railway', the latter referring to the original ownership of that line. H. C. CASSERLEY

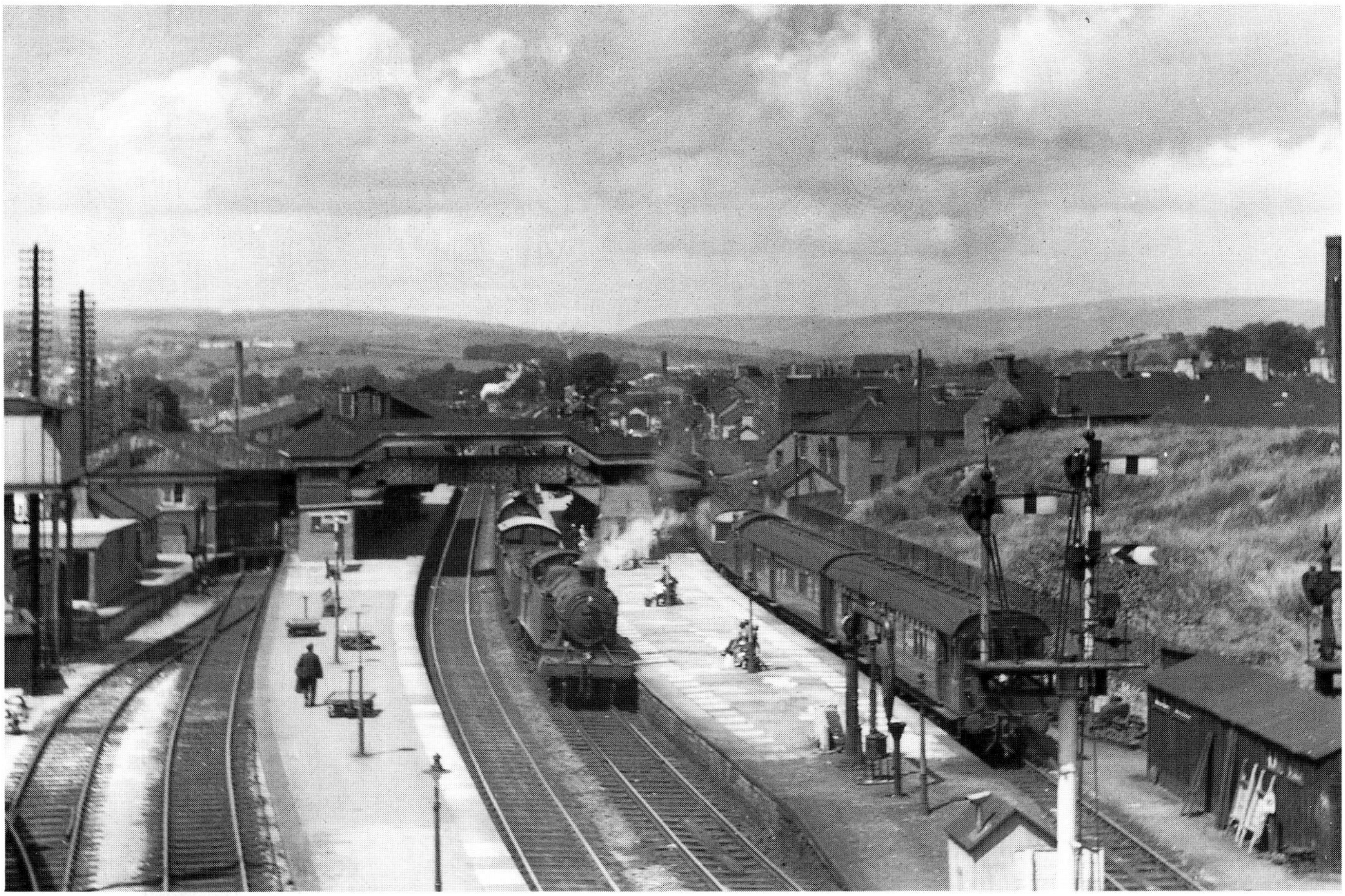

This photograph of Bridgend from the roadbridge at the east end of the station, on 3rd July 1954, provides a good view of the main lines through the station, with the Barry bay to the left, and the Valleys platform on the right. Ebbw Jct. 2–8–2T No. 7243 is seen running through the station with an up class 'H' freight, while a '45XX' was working a 3-car auto service to the Valleys, the nearer vehicles being ex-Taff Vale driving trailer No. W2501 (formerly No. 354) and W6423 (ex-TVR No. 80), with a GWR trailer beyond the engine. S. RICKARD

The Up 'South Wales Pullman' (4.30 p.m. Swansea to Paddington) standing at the up platform at Bridgend Station on Wednesday, 2nd March 1960 behind Landore 'Castle' No. 5091 *Cleeve Abbey*. No. 5091 had been through a Heavy General repair just five weeks previously, and was still in pristine condition. The engine worked through to Paddington with the Pullman, returning the following morning with the 8.55 a.m. Paddington to Pembroke Dock service as far as Swansea. The west-bound Pullman train left Paddington at 8.50 a.m., Saturdays excepted. F. K. DAVIES, CTY. G. W. TRUST

Another view of the east end of Bridgend station, this time from the down platform, about 1963. The platform furniture was still almost entirely Great Western, and there had been little change to the structures since the final years of the old company. However, the comprehensive station nameboard had been replaced by a standard metal board simply proclaiming 'Bridgend'.
LENS OF SUTTON

The last Standard Class '9', No. 92250, with Giesel ejector, passing through Bridgend with a down class 'H' train of empty mineral wagons on 8th June 1963. At this time, the engine was allocated to Newport (Ebbw Jct.) shed. F. K. DAVIES, CTY. G. W. TRUST

This picture of Old Oak Common 'Castle' No. 5082 *Swordfish* provides a good view of Bridgend goods shed and the line ahead to the north-west of Bridgend on Friday, 6th May 1960. The train was the 11.55 a.m. Paddington to West Wales service due into Bridgend at 3.19 p.m., with through coaches to Pembroke Dock and Milford Haven with the restaurant car section running through to Swansea. The group of men making their way from the platform to the shed were probably the local LDC members returning from a meeting at Cardiff. F. K. DAVIES, CTY. G. W. TRUST

The 10.15 am. Carmarthen to Cheltenham running into Bridgend behind Landore 'Hall' No. 4910 *Blaisdon Hall* on 23rd November 1957. On the LDR 36 roster, the engine ran this train to Cardiff, and returned with the 9.10 a.m. Manchester (2.29 p.m. Cardiff) to Swansea. The coaching stock was a four-coach corridor set with strengthening and vans attached; it ran much further afield than the locomotive, working a Swansea, Carmarthen, Cheltenham and Swindon route on the first day, and a Swindon, Hereford, Gloucester, Cardiff and Swansea on the second. The flat barrows on the down platform were a common type of platform equipment at this time, and a less-than-comfortable seat for many an enthusiast.

Neath 'Hall' No. 4967 *Shirenewton Hall* approaching the station from the west with an up express on 7th July 1962. The engine had spent several months in store over the winter of 1961/2, and had been allocated to Neath the previous month; it was condemned two months after this photograph was taken on 7th September. Bridgend Middle box can be seen on the extreme right, with associated signals.

S. RICKARD

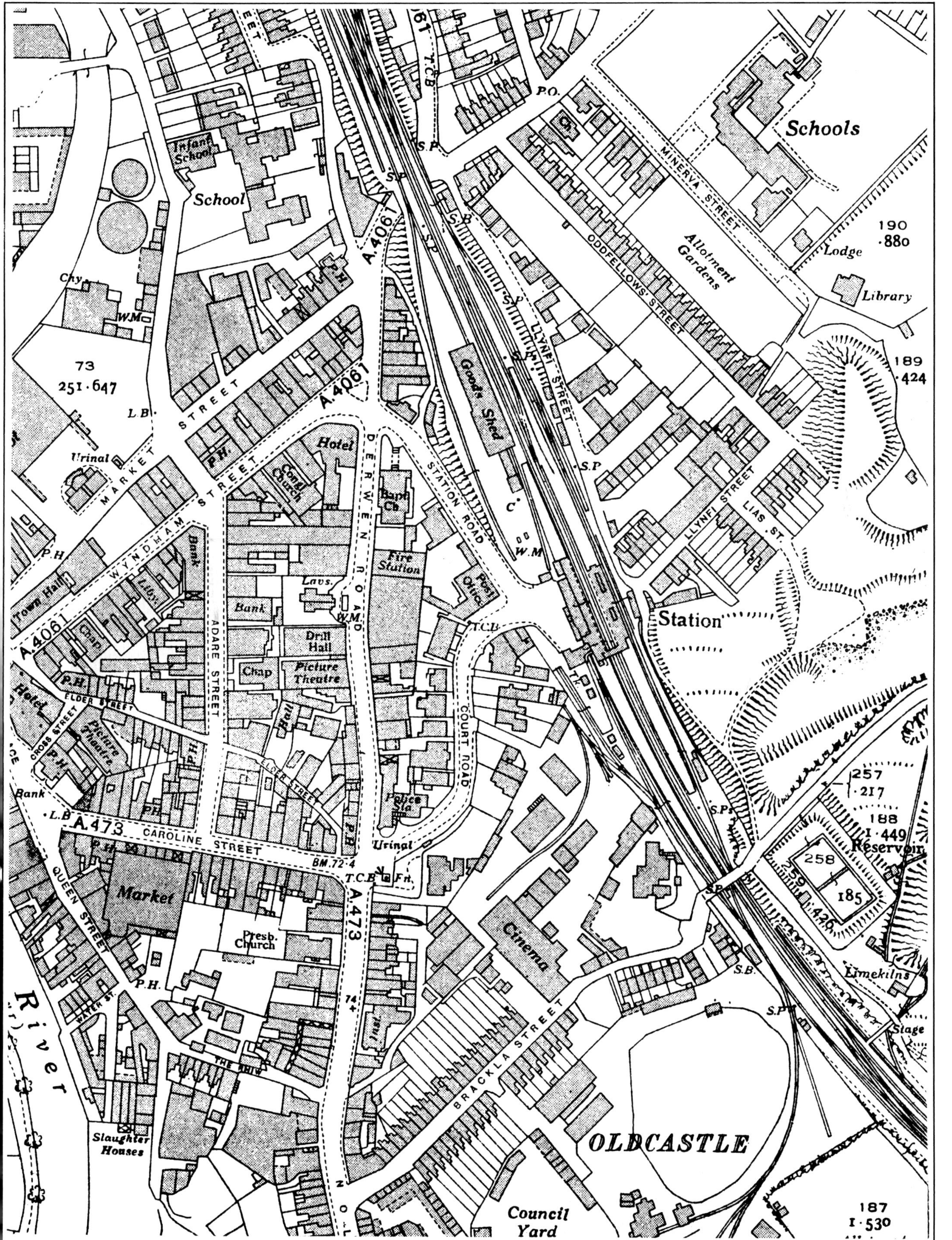

Taken from 25-inch Ordnance Survey for 1940. (Crown copyright reserved)

With the summer sun high in the sky to the south, this picture shows Landore 'Castle' No. 7021 *Haverfordwest Castle* with the 11.15 a.m. Swansea to Manchester service, Train M72, running into Bridgend past the goods shed. Having been a Landore engine since her introduction into traffic in June 1949, No. 7021 remained in the West Wales area when that depot closed, being transferred to Old Oak Common on 11th January 1962, and is seen here with an '81A' shedplate on 7th July 1962.

S. RICKARD

The Valleys platform occupied by Tondu's No. 9649, on a 2-coach service, probably to Nantymoel, again on 7th July 1962. The Tondu and Valleys route had its own line out of the Valleys platform, running northwards out of the station alongside the up main; it joined the double-track line to Tondu beyond Middle signal box.
S. RICKARD

Tondu 2–6–2T No. 5555 standing at the Valleys platform, Bridgend, with a train to the Llynfi Valley on 23rd November 1957; this platform was the north face of the island platform, and served passenger trains to the Llynfi (Abergwynfi) and Ogmore (Nantymoel) Valleys, and in earlier years to the Garw Valley (Blaengarw) and Gilfach Goch lines too. The '45XX' and its train ran through Tondu and Maesteg to Abergwynfi, a journey of some 14 miles that took about 45 minutes.

An unusual routeing for an up freight service. The Middle box signalman had apparently taken advantage of a clear Valleys platform to accept this eastbound class 'H' freight, probably from Margam, headed by Tondu (88H) '42XX' No. 5208, to await a clear road to proceed after a following up main-line passenger, on Saturday, 7th July 1962.
S. RICKARD